Adventures of a 21st-Century Dowser

by John Baker

Foreword by
John Barnes
Detective Inspector – Retired

Quicksilver Publications

First published in the United Kingdom in 2008 by
Quicksilver Publications – quicksilver7@btinternet.com

ISBN 978-0-9557600-1-3

Typeset in 11/14 pt Arial
Typesetting by Heather Ellis – heatherellis123@yahoo.co.uk
Origination by Patricia J Mills – quicksilver7@btinternet.com
Printed in England by J.H. Haynes & Co. Ltd, Sparkford, Somerset.

Foreword

Originally John was a neighbour of ours before our move to Cambridgeshire from Kent. It was on one of his weekends visiting us after our move that the word 'dowsing' entered the conversation. By the strangest of coincidences, I had recently bought some old books and the one I had been reading just before his visit was *Dowsing, The Art of Rhabdomancy* by Robert H Leftwich.

Before anyone gets arrested, you should know the dictionary definition of Rhabdomancy is 'divination by means of a rod or wand, esp. in discovering ores, springs of water, etc.'

We turned to the book to see what was needed to get started, and it just seemed to be a couple of metal rods fashioned into L-shapes. The rest was up to us.

My wife, John and I then tried our hand at dowsing in the drive beside the house, with varying degrees of success. John seemed to take to it like a duck to water and we have had several dowsing adventures since, one of which is featured in this book.

John Barnes, Detective Inspector – Retired
Elm, Cambridge

P.S. I still dabble in dowsing, as does my wife Elizabeth, who is better at it than me. I should add that I am proud to be 'Maker of Rods' to one John Baker.

Preface

I have been dowsing for over twelve years now and enjoy every aspect of it. I am constantly learning new ways to obtain information and improving the way I pose a question in order to get a more reliable answer, thus becoming more accurate. People often ask, "How does it work?", but it's difficult to explain to those who can't do it.

Although others may think differently, in my opinion and experience, the human mind seems to have access to its own worldwide web of information. Rather like tuning in a radio to a specific wavelength, I tune in to what I am looking for. For example, I may be walking across a field looking for the sub-surface remains of a sixteenth-century building. If it is there, I will find it and be able to plot its layout, but if some seventeenth-century additions were made, I would not find them until I started looking for something built in the seventeenth century. You may find this difficult to take on board but that is what happens.

Dowsing for the date of an artefact is another phenomenon. The calendar and dating were introduced by man in order to give historical perspective to our time on earth. So where does this information come from?

In the same way, it is possible to dowse whether a certain person lived in a certain dwelling. We go back to the worldwide web. It is argued that everything and everyone that ever existed leaves behind a signal or remanence which it is possible to tune in to. This is subtle to the nth degree but that is part of how I believe dowsing works.

John Baker

To Rosemary

Acknowledgements

Trish Mills, without whose help this book would not have appeared.
Mr and Mrs C. Papworth
Chris Baker (no relation), Director, and members of the Dartford District Archaeology Group
John and Elizabeth Barnes
Roger Cockett, Director, Fawkham and Ash Archaeology Group
'Amy'
Hugh Nisbet
Brian Edwards
Anne Leonard MA www.opnewworld.co.uk
Jim and Bette Studd
Victoria Baxter
John Moss, Director, and staff at the BSD office, Malvern
Col John Blashford-Snell www.ses-explore.org
José Alexandre Cotta of Radiesthesia Lusitania, Portugal
Brian Edwards
Flame Television Productions
Royal Engineers Library, Chatham
Gordon Ingram, Convener, Heritage Writtle
Bill and Kath Jordan
Beth Reeve
Ken Walton
With apologies to anyone missed out.

CHAPTER ONE

First, Some History

Without water, life on our planet could not exist. Wherever early man roamed, he needed to find water that was safe to drink. Rivers seem an obvious place, but they were often polluted by animals and peoples further upstream. Wild animals also drank from rivers, and this would have been an added danger.

In each settlement or community there was probably someone who, through the sheer necessity to survive, had an ability to find water. Springs were one source but they could dry up and do not occur everywhere.

With man's discovery of fire, impure water could be boiled and made safe to drink, but as man began to domesticate cattle and settle down from a more nomadic existence, a larger and more regular supply of water was needed to sustain livestock, simple farming and the population. In those times, dowsing for water would be treated as a commonplace function. Indeed, many of today's farmers regard it simply as a useful tool.

Over the centuries, wars and invasions became part of the human condition and the first thing an army of occupation needed was a supply of drinking water for men and animals. Often, retreating armies would poison wells so new supplies had to be found quickly. Dowsing for water was no big deal, and was often the only way to source a new supply.

During the reign of Queen Elizabeth I there were people in Central Europe who were dowsing for various mineral deposits and

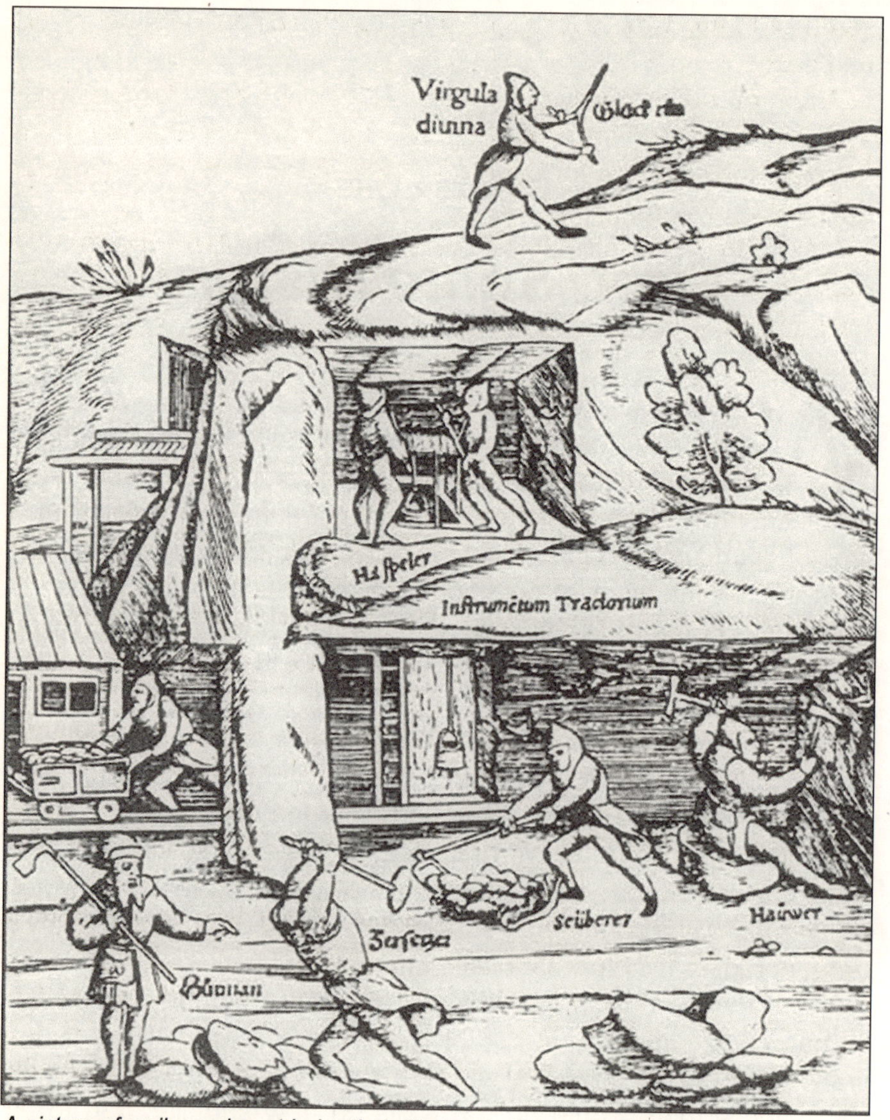

A picture of a silver mine at Leberthal, Alsace, in France. Reproduced from Cosmographic Universalis *by Sebastian Munster of Basle, published in 1550. You will note there is a gentleman prospecting for more silver at the top of the hill, using a forked twig. Is this early evidence of divining? 'Virgula' is apparently Latin for 'little twig' or 'divining rod'.*

some of them came over to England to search for deposits of ore and coal.

During the Crimean war, typhoid and dysentery took more allied lives than did cannon or rifle fire. It would have been worse if one Sapper Kelly had not dowsed for - and found - clean water, thus enabling new wells to be dug.

After the Second World War, the British Army became a permanent feature in what became West Germany and the water supply at their base in Mönchengladbach was discovered by Col H. Grattan. He explored the local heathland on horseback, dowsing for a water supply that would be safe from enemy interference. This water source, which is still in use today, is separate from the local German water supply and is of a better quality.

In 1933, members of the Royal Engineers formed a dowsing group which has evolved into the British Society of Dowsers. Until the year 2000, its presidents were usually ex-army.

After visiting the Royal Engineers' library at Chatham in Kent, I discovered in their magazine, *The Journal*, numerous articles from outposts all over the British Empire about the successfull use of dowsing.

There is an interesting piece by Major D.P. Cadoux-Hudson RE, which ends with the following sentence: 'The fact remains that it works and in an age of increasing complexity and technology, it is refreshing to find a detector which is simple, soldier-proof and at the same time highly accurate, and that it can be made from only three feet of g 1098 wire or demolition cable.'

Today, dowsers are in greater demand than ever. Water is becoming an expensive and increasingly rare commodity and a good water diviner can earn a healthy living not just in the UK but worldwide. If you can find water, you can find other things too, so why restrict dowsing to just water? I recently heard of someone who dowsed for and found a large oil leak in a big transfer pipe after the company concerned had spent several months trying to establish its location.

My dowsing mentor, the late and much missed Dan Wilson, was a highly qualified engineer who did the final checks on large transmitters for ITT. Management discovered that compared to other people doing this, almost none of the ones that Dan had checked ever suffered a breakdown. So he was asked how he did it, and he told them he simply dowsed the circuitry for faults. Management laughed, but that is what he did. His skills improved his reliability but the Company was not interested in having him teach other inspectors.

For some years now, archaeologists have been using dowsing to find sub-surface structures and artefacts. It is not something they broadcast for fear of being ridiculed by their colleagues, but the boot should be on the other foot. In 1988 a book written by Prof. Richard Bailey called *Dowsing and Church Archaeology*, showed that dowsing brought to light a number of things not noted by other means, and which were subsequently verified.

Published in 1993, *Techniques of Archaeology* by Phil Baker (no relation) advocated the use of dowsing when other means of investigation were not possible.The question 'Why not dowse in the first place?' does not seem to have occurred to anyone!

Slowly, perceptions of dowsing are changing and some universities now offer dowsing modules relating to sub-surface features. Archeaologists use resistivity machines and ground penetrating radar, all very technical and expensive, but in my opinion, the best bit of kit is between their ears, costs nothing and, with practice, is highly reliable. Let's hope that one day they wake up to its potential.

Chapter Two

My Story

It's not often that your whole life can be turned upside down by a chance remark over lunch. On a summer's day in East Anglia, for some reason the word dowsing came up.

"Aha!" said my hosts, John and Elizabeth Barnes, "we have a book upstairs which has a chapter on just that subject. We'll go and get it." And they did.

I was confronted by a picture of an elderly gentleman wearing a soppy hat and holding two bent metal rods like a pair of six guns. Despite my protestations, by majority vote it was decided that 'we' should have a go. My idea of spending the afternoon on a sun lounger with a ready supply of iced gin and tonic to hand was rapidly fading.

A quick trip to a local industrial estate and the purchase of a couple of lengths of metal rod, soon meant that John had made up two pairs of these rods. One pair was thrust into my hands and, feeling rather silly, I was to be the guinea pig in the first dowsing trial, which was to walk down their drive and see what happened.

A few paces later, these bits of metal swung across me in no uncertain manner. We all looked at each other open mouthed. Wow, what was that all about?

I was told to go back and do it again and, sure enough, at the same spot the rods crossed, yet I had done nothing but hold them. This was most curious.

"Do you know what's under there?" asked John.

"Not a clue," I replied.

"That," he said, "is where the water pipe crosses the drive to the greenhouse."

I was persuaded to go a bit further and a few yards on the rods swung outwards. This was getting more intriguing by the minute. Again, the question, "Do you know what that is?" Well of course I didn't.

"That," said John, "is where the electricity cable, within a protective pipe, crosses the drive to power the driveway lights."

I needed a gin and tonic and fast. As I recall, John then had a go with mixed results. Elizabeth found the water pipe but not the electric one. At this point three bemused people retired to the sun loungers in the garden. This needed thinking about.

The following day I tried it again on my own patch, and the same things happened. In other parts of my garden the rods would move, sometimes a little and sometimes a lot. It was as if they had a life of their own. I had to find out more. I wandered through the house holding the rods and they moved at certain points where it seemed central heating and water pipes travelled under the floor. In the back garden they opened out at one point. The question was, what was really going on and was there anybody out there who could help?

There was. I telephoned an organisation called the British Society of Dowsers (BSD), explained what was happening, and they offered to have someone contact me. Days later, I was visited by a Dan Wilson, who put me through my paces and told me that what I was picking up in the garden was a black line. These black lines, he said, were not nice if they ended up under your house, as they tended to make people ill, but this one was passing through, so not to worry.

It seemed that I had some natural ability to dowse and he encouraged me to take it further. He then told me he didn't do that sort of dowsing, his speciality was healing.

"Oh, that's handy," I said. "I have terrible trouble with sciatica."

My back, knee and heel were all painful and I had seen a doctor, a physiotherapist and an osteopath, all to no avail. Dan promptly offered to give me some healing. He said the original cause was that when I was thirteen, I had fallen and banged my head. I thought for a moment and remembered that it had happened, and probably about that age. How did he know?!

So there I was, sitting with a complete stranger holding my foot and quivering slightly, while I was trying to take it all in. After about ten minutes, he put my foot back on the floor and said I should get some relief soon, and if it had not cleared up in ten days, to telephone him. With that he left.

That night I slept as I had never slept before, really deeply, and the next morning I immediately noticed that the pain under my heel was almost gone. Over the next few days the knee pain disappeared too but my back still wasn't right.

There had been no talk of money during all this, but I wanted to pay for the relief it brought me, so I contacted him again and asked how much he charged. He said, if I was happy to give it, £25 would be appreciated.

Believe me, it was more than good value. For the next few years, Dan became my mentor and I discovered how fortunate I was to know such a remarkable person.

So, there I was, an embryo dowser and into something which could include healing. This was getting more fascinating by the minute. There must be a local group I could join. Time to start asking around.

I could find nothing in London or Kent, which surprised me a little, so I decided to join the British Society of Dowsers (BSD), in order to learn more. It also meant I could place an advertisement in their journal, asking if anyone was interested in forming a London group, would they contact me.

In the meantime, I visited my local church which is part Norman with a large graveyard, in order to get some quiet and unobserved practise. Some chance! There were people using the paths as short cuts; there were people tending graves; and there were visitors to the church itself; it really was busy. Still feeling self-conscious wandering about with two pieces of bent metal in my hands, this was not what I expected. There were a lot of other things about to manifest themselves that I had not expected either.

I had brought along a few canes to use as markers and, walking along the front of the church, at four distinct points the rods swung outwards. This signal must mean some kind of energy, so I placed a cane to mark each spot, and then walked the same area but further away from the church. Again, the four signals cropped up, but a greater distance apart. Again I marked each spot and repeated the exercise even further away, with the same results.

Using line of sight, I noticed that all four lines of canes appeared to be converging on one corner of the church tower. I went to the other side of the tower to see if the lines fanned out again, but had no reaction at all. Over the years it has been explained to me that I may have picked up positive energy but not negative, and that the lines probably did fan out on the other side, even though I could not find them.

I went to the stand pipe where visitors could collect water for their flower vases, and seemed to follow the line of the pipe through the churchyard, but I had no proof.

On another visit, as I was passing a yew tree, both rods swung across me and pointed to the tree. On walking round it, I found the rods would swing in about fiteen times. As I walked towards the trunk, the rods crossed as I approached.

Having been told that ley lines often run through the tops of hills and ancient sites, I looked for one of those. There did seem to be a ley line running through the church. If I walked the same path asking to be shown a water pipe, the ley line did not register. So it was dependent on what you were looking for and the questions you asked.

If seemed if you tuned in to a specific item, and if it was there, you would pick it up, but if other things were also there, they did not show until you tuned in to them. It was starting to make sense but these reactions seemed impossible to prove. Was it just my imagination playing tricks? I had to find some way of getting proof.

My advertisement brought in one page of Basildon Bond and a postcard. Sue and Allen wanted to join a Group, but in the whole of London, no one else. We arranged a meeting and at the last minute Sue could not make it, so two of us sat in a pub to decide what to do next.

All I wanted to do was join something. I did not want to have any official capacity. Neither did Allen, but there were only three players and one of those was missing. So eventually it was reluctantly agreed that Allen would be Honorary Secretary and, by default, I would be Chairman, of the grandly named London and Thamesside Dowsers (LTD!). We needed a Treasurer. On being asked, Sue declined the invitation, but as we had no money, it didn't really matter. We arranged to have our first meeting at the Barbican centre café in London.

Having received my first BSD Journal, I was interested to discover that apart from water divining, there were other things such as earth energies, references to Michael and Mary lines, psychometry (dating artefacts) and map dowsing. That looked interesting, it would save a lot of time being stared at and wandering around fields. I would have to have a go at that. My idea of an exciting moment would be to find some old building that I could dowse and then get proof that it was there.

I had always been interested in archaeology and had once done a dig in the garden of my parents' pub. With growing excitement I had found some old tiles. On the back was some marking and, rubbing off the mud, I saw the letter L - or was it a Roman number? A bit more rubbing and an M appeared. That was a Roman numeral too. Wow! This was getting better by the minute. I rushed indoors and put the tile under the tap and eventually the word MARLEY appeared. My heart sank but the original feeling of excitement has stayed with me. I had to find a way to get involved with the local archaeologists.

The first meeting of the London and Thamesside Dowsers took place at the Barbican and all three members were present. Sue was into healing and Allen favoured water divining, so we had a long talk on both subjects.

Over a period of a year, one or two new members joined but our venue was not ideal and we could not afford to hire a room. One day, a chap whose ears and nose were impaled by bits of architectural ironmongery turned up. He was a multimedia artist who, amongst other things, did something with lighted candles. Now don't get carried away here, I saw the pictures and was impressed. These were taken at shows and art events. He was an extremely gifted individual and designed the logo for our Group.

I soon contacted my local archaeology group and found that their secretary also dowsed. He offered to take me to a local field where the remains of an eighteenth-century building were evident through discolouration in the grass. This was ideal training as it gave me confidence that what I was picking up was actually there. The problem with this group was that, being in a fairly built-up area, no actual digging was going on.

From time to time I tried map dowsing, but it did not seem to work for me until one day I saw a programme on television about two men who had got themselves trapped on the Eiger in Switzerland. A dowser was working from a local map to try to establish their position and, based on this information, a mountain rescue team went out and found them, saving their lives. Encouraged by this, I had another go the following day, and it actually seemed to work. This was a major step forward.

My next foray into dowsing was to contact Dartford and District Archaeological Group (DDAG) and ask their Director, Chris Baker (no relation), if I could do some dowsing with them as I wanted to improve my abilty. I had been told that professional archaeologists had no time for dowsers, so how would I fare with an amateur group? It so happened that the DDAG were on a site dig and yes, I could come along to practise. This was wonderful news. I'd read about digs, seen them on television and now I was to get the chance to actually go on site.

On my first visit, I was met with a certain amount of curiosity, but allowed to wander at will. The site consisted of a series of graves about eight feet deep. Not having looked for graves before, I found this an interesting challenge.

Wandering about the sloping site, I picked up two energy lines that ran down the slope about 15 feet apart. I marked them on a plan I was preparing and over the coming weeks became more involved with the digging side.

My search for other graves was not totally successful. I seemed to find adult burials but not those of children. I had been told by my mentor, Dan, that I should also be able to get a date for when the people had been buried. I tried this and got a date of about 640 AD for Saxon burials. Later I was told that they were indeed of the Saxon period, so that pleased me.

I had often pondered about the yew tree in the cemetery and why my rods were attracted to it. I was told that the yew was revered in past centuries as it lived for hundreds of years and was often planted over a blind spring. A blind spring does not have the power to bubble up to the surface. Long ago diviners would find them and, as water was vital for life and the yew had a long life, the two together became a place of worship. People often ask why yew trees are found in churchyards. The question really should be why are churchyards full of yew trees? The answer is that the yew was probably there long before Christianity reached these shores.

Things were starting to make sense now. Dowsing was all about looking for something specific. It was possible to find something underground, measure it, establish its age, and how deep down it was. It seemed that almost anything was possible and the more you practised, the better you became. I was hooked by now and being invited out by other people to look for things.

When I was dowsing in a field, I sometimes had the feeling that someone was watching me. Out of the corner of my eye I could just see what looked like a dark net curtain and the vague appearance of a face behind it. If I turned to look at it, it would disappear, but would return a few minutes later. I was also aware of another feeling but could not put my finger on it. It was a few years before I would get the answer.

In the meantime, I was wandering in the gardens of some almshouses which had been built long before a piped water supply would have been available. There seemed to be two wells quite close together and I tried to find out how deep they were. I also wanted to know when they fell into disuse and was given a date of 1353 for both of them. Sometime later I was told that the plague arrived in England in 1349, so maybe people using the wells had died of that. I also tried to find out if the wells were ever brought back into use and received a negative answer.

Whilst concentrating on my search, I looked across at another garden which was laid to lawn, and 'saw' another well. I turned to the people I was with and said, "There's another well over there." To my eyes at least, I could clearly see a well. It had rough black stonework at the top and its sides appeared as grey. Of course, no one else could see it and they all looked somewhat surprised that I could. I looked away and back again, and it had gone.

Nevertheless, getting permission sometime later to go into the next garden, and having made a mental note of the spot, I did pick up the outline of a well and guess what? The same date for its disuse cropped up.

My knowledge of history is pretty poor. All my history teachers at school seemed to have one objective in mind, which was to bore us to death in the shortest possible time. Yet history is a vibrant subject, as I have subsequently discovered. My lack of knowledge is in some ways an advantage, as when I am dowsing for a date or time scale, the information I am getting is honest and not coloured by my own source of conscious information.

The almshouses were close to the church with the yew tree, so I went back to it and started dowsing again, this time for water. As I approached the trunk, the rods crossed, so there did seem to be a spring beneath it, at a depth of about 12 feet. Sometime in the past, someone had known of this and the yew tree was planted. I investigated other yews in the vicinity with no response at all.

I had been invited to visit another local archaeological group to see if I could find an old manor house. In a large sloping field with a church at the bottom stood Roger Cockett, complete with theodelite and graph paper, to make notes on my progress. My thinking was that if I had a manor house, I would like a view, so I started at the top of the field and gradually worked down to Roger at the bottom. At last I was picking up something and started marking out the area with canes. I ended up with a nice chunky square and a small extension to one side. Roger was measuring it all off and that, we thought, was that.

* * * * *

A number of dowsing courses were advertised in the BSD Journal and I decided to join one being held at Regent's Park College in London. It was a beginners course and included the subject of non-retinal vision, which sounded interesting. The course was to be run by a retired GP, Renee Puddefoot.

The Regent's Park College course began with dowsing techniques and I was pleased to learn that, largely self-taught though I was, I had the basics right. The second part was non-retinal dowsing. We were all blindfolded then told a story about a Belgian stage illusionist who had discovered by accident that he seemed to have unusual powers, and we were going to try and do what he had done.

Blindfolded and on our honour, we could feel an envelope on the desk in front of us, and had to take out the top sheet of paper. By running our hands across it, or holding it to our foreheads, we had to guess the colour of it. We all had random colours so it was up to us to decide our colour. We were tested on three colours – a small choice – then three papers with a number from 0 to 99 written on it, and finally three pages with a simple picture on each one.

FAWKHAM AND ASH ARCHAEOLOGICAL GROUP

Hon Secretary: E P Connell — Excavations Director: R A C Cockett

Gravesend
Kent

John Baker Esq
68 Iron Mill Lane
Crayford
Kent DA1 4RR

24 March 1997

Dear John

DOWSING/DIVINING EXERCISE AT FAWKHAM

Here (at last!) are copies of the survey plot of your predicted wall positions, printed on paper and of the 1966 excavation plan, printed on a transparency. C1-C2 on each survey represents the east wall of the chancel of Fawkham parish church, so you should begin by superimposing the transparency over the paper. You will see that your results certainly do overlap the excavated building, so that if we had dug where you indicated, we should have found the building.

However the plans are clearly a long way out of alignment. The intriguing thing however is that if you now rotate the transparency clockwise, there is quite a close fit between the two. This obviously invites the thought that either the 1966 survey or my 1997 survey is wrong with respect to the church, but right with respect to the buried building. However I have made careful checks on each, and neither seems to be inaccurate.

So let's have another go (or rather two more goes) in Kingsdown on Easter Monday! In addition to the manor house near Kingsdown church, the foundations of another manor house in Kingsdown exist beneath the surface of a recreation ground up there. We could possibly get through both of them in a busy morning, but if you are able to stay there with us into the afternoon next Monday, so much the better. See you there about 10am. Let us hope for good results. A route map is enclosed.

Yours sincerely

Roger

ROGER COCKETT

A letter arrived from Roger Cockett.

Just running my hands over the paper, not even touching it, I could definitely sense something. We called out what we thought was on our individual sheets of paper. My first impression of one of my pictures was of a heart, but on second thoughts I decided it was an apple. Here I'm going to cheat a little, because I claim four successes out of nine: two colours, one number and my apple *was* a heart, so I take that as a plus since, sideways on, an apple can look very much like a heart shape. I was quite impressed with myself, especially the picture, as that could have been of anything. As to what success the others had, I have no idea, being so taken up with my own experience.

After two years the London dowsing group now had about six members. They were interesting people, but what we needed was a decent meeting place and that happened when a certain Guy Holmes joined us. An ex-Royal Marine Commando, he had extricated his Troop out of serious trouble when, on winter manouvres in Norway, they lost their tents and equipment when a night-time storm blew up. He dowsed the direction required to get his Troop back to base, and started off, getting back three hours before another Troop in similar circumstances had managed it.

Guy and his Dutch wife, Leisbet, invited us to use their house for our bi-monthly meetings. Our new venue was in Mile End with constant supplies of tea and coffee, while members brought biscuits and cake. Guy also became treasurer, so with some money in the kitty, we could invite people in to give us talks. This was a major step forward.

A letter arrived from Roger Cockett and with it a scale plan of my dowsed layout of the manor house, together with another plan of the building. Apparently the site had already been investigated as a dig. So that was why he stayed at the bottom of the slope. I was being tested! My layout was five degrees out from his original plan, but if you placed the two on top of each other, they were a perfect match!

Roger was keen for me to check some other sites and, over the next twelve months I think I tramped over half the county with him

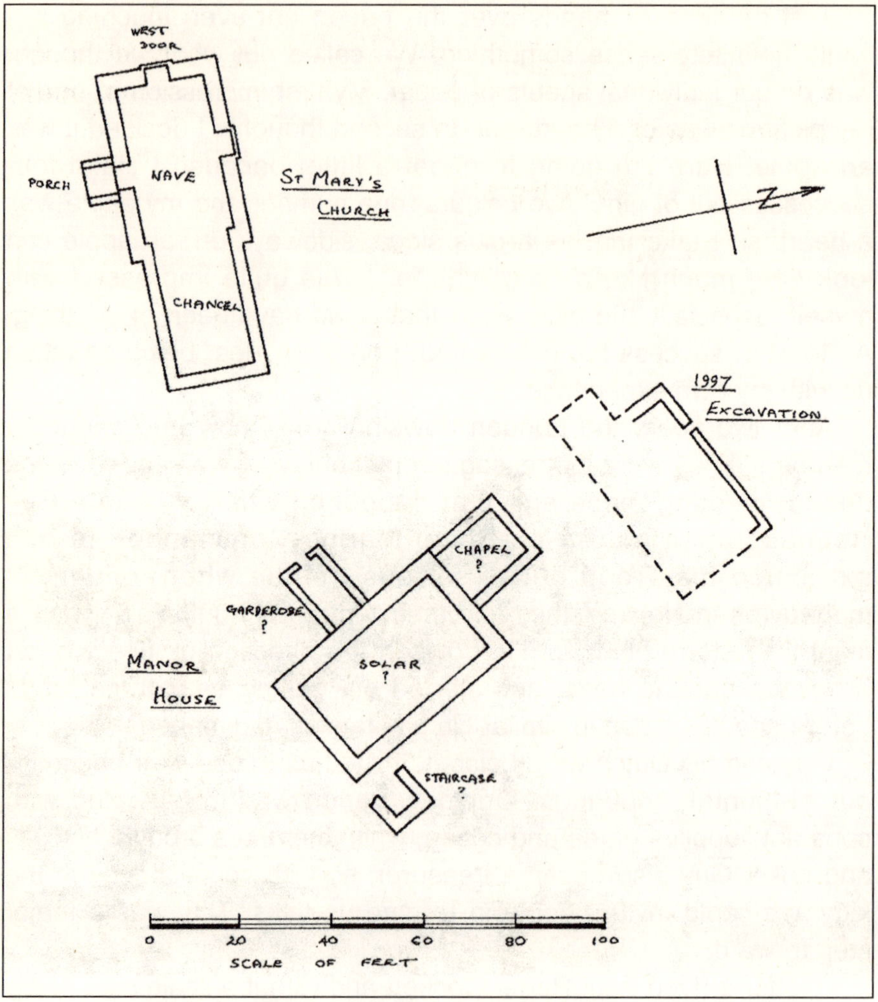

Above: *An outline plan of Fawkham Manor, showing St Mary's Church and the manorial buildings excavated in 1964 and 1997, as it appears in the Fawkham and Ash Archaeological Group's booklet,* The Story of Fawkham Manor.

Opposite page:
John's initial plan, based on his dowsed findings before he was even told what he was looking for! Says John, "My layout was five degrees out from the original plan, but if you placed the two on top of each other, they were a perfect match!"

Note: Both plans are aligned due north.

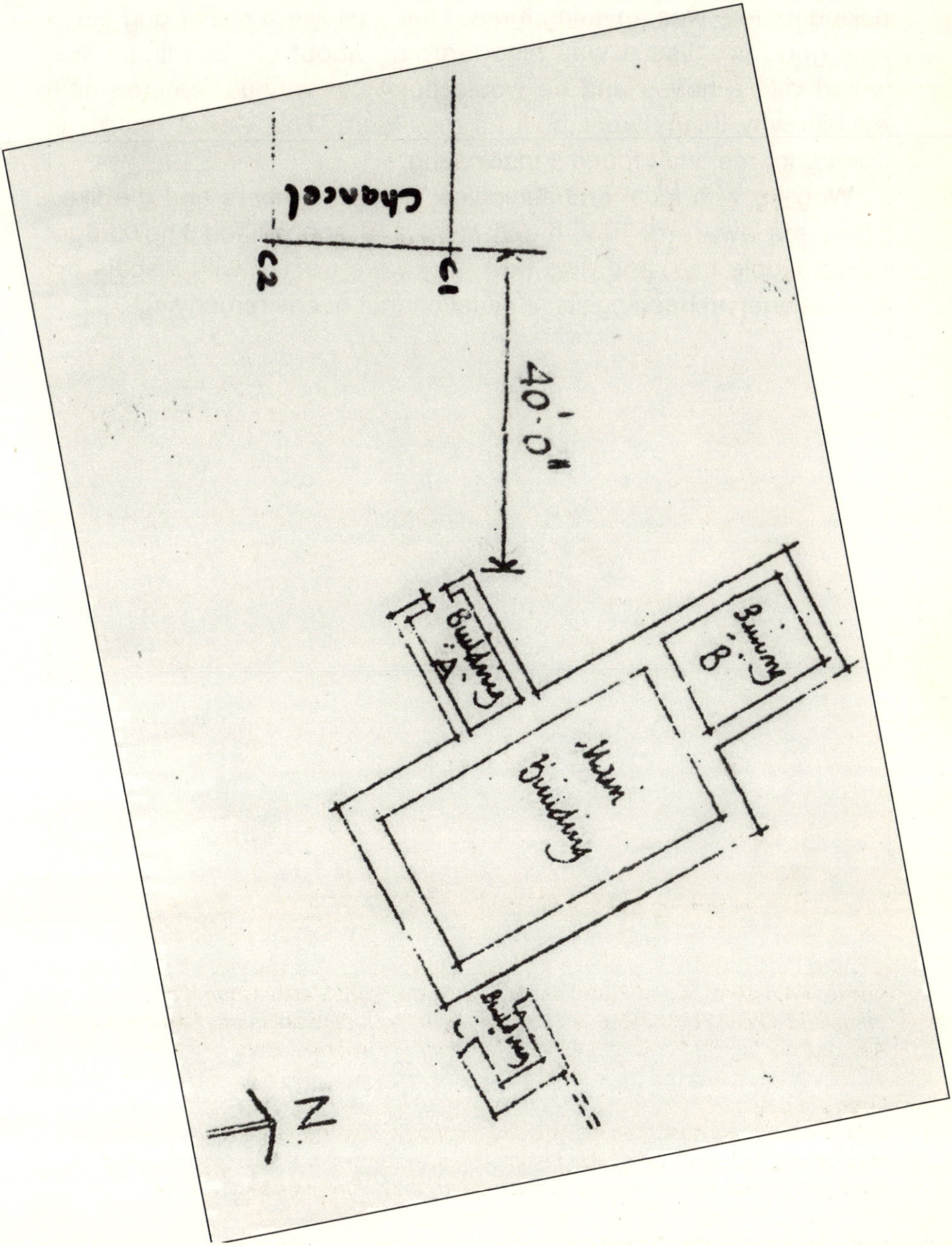
Chancel
C1
C2
40'-0"
Building 'A'
Building 'B'
Main Building
N

asking if there was anything there. I felt a bit like a sniffer dog but it was good practise. I was also learning about old buildings. We would visit a house and he would point out various features and explain why things were built as they were. This was a real eye-opener for me and I found it fascinating.

Working with local archaeological group members and the like, I became aware of how much local and specialised knowledge these people had, and also how they were treated with disdain by professional archaeologists, a situation that needs remedying.

CHAPTER THREE

The Energy Line Mystery

Twelve or so years of dowsing have been a life-changing experience. My view on life and my attitude to it has changed dramatically. I seem to be more aware of things, as if the blinkers have come off, and I can see the bigger picture. So far it has all been an adventure into the unknown. Was it now going to get boring? If only I had known. The last thing it was going to be was boring!

One morning I received a telephone call from Chris Baker, telling me that the lines I had marked on the layout as coming down the slope of the hill had been uncovered by a professional archaeological group, who had begun to investigate the site. They had stripped the topsoil using a machine. This did not seem to make sense as the lines had seemed to me to be about energy, and you can't 'see' energy, just its effects.

Intrigued, I went to the site and sure enough, spaced about 15 feet apart, were two lines of sand and gravel going straight down the hill. I showed my original sketch to the lady in charge of the dig and she was surprised in a low-key sort of way. Apart from the two lines, the rest of the hillside had been exposed down to its chalk base.

Looking in more detail at the lines, they emanated from the hill-top plateau and looked as though they carried water down the slope in two rivulets, hence the sand and gravel. But why did they give me the idea that this was energy? I'm nothing if not curious, and set about asking various people as to what would give that effect?

Eventually I discovered that chalk is a bad conductor of electricity. Therefore, natural energy would seek a conductor in order to move from place to place. And here the path of least resistance was down the two rivulets, hence my straight lines. They *were* energy lines, natural earth energy, and I doubt I will ever find such an example again. I have not read of anything similar being dowsed or discovered since then either. It was quite amazing.

About this time I decided it would be a good idea to go to the annual BSD Congress. Time to feed my thirst for more knowledge and meet potential prospects to come and give a talk to our London Group, two or three members of which were also there, as was Dan Wilson.

One of the talks at the Congress was given by a GP on the Bach flower remedies. I was surprised by the number of professional people attending, many of them of some standing. In fact, I was beginning to wonder if I was getting out of my depth. I met an astronomer, several GPs, architects and some surveyors. I was not aware of any archaeologists present, which seemed a pity and which I did not understand.

To my mind, the majority of people at the Congress represented a fair cross-section from many different walks of life. Sensible and knowledgeable to say the least, with very few you could accuse of having odd views or going to extremes. There again, perhaps people would say I was developing odd views myself. They certainly did not seem odd to me. They were and are views based on first-hand experience and I had certainly questioned them myself before feeling comfortable with them.

My favourite moment of the Congress weekend was at a workshop where one of the instructors put an invisible ley line across the floor and we had to find it, which we did! He then removed it and we had to try to find it again, but it had gone. Now that was something I had to try at home.

On the back of that I bought a book written by Alfred Watkins called *The Old Straight Track*, which I found hard going. The author believes these lines are the original 'roads' put down by early man to get about through the dense forest covering the country at that time. He further believed that it is possible to 'find' them today. I have no problem with finding them but as to their origin and use, I am still not sure.

The whole Congress was most enjoyable. I left feeling I needed a couple of days off to get over what was both a hectic and tiring time. Plus the fact that there were other facets of dowsing of which I had been unaware, and which I was determined to investigate.

CHAPTER FOUR

Hunting for heiffers X marks the spot

I was off to the Barnes household for a weekend away and a change of scenery. Just after breakfast on the Saturday morning, all was quiet and I was looking forward to cutting some grass with their sit-and-ride tractor, when the telephone rang. My ears pricked up when I heard John saying to someone, "We are on our way." Who, I think to myself, is 'we'. You've guessed it, 'we' is me.

Apparently two heifers had escaped from a farmer's field and help was needed to round them up. Jumping in my car, off we raced to the farm. Driving along I asked, "How big are these animals?"

"Oh, they're only small," grinned John reassuringly. Reaching the farm I was confronted with a contingent of cloth-capped Wellington-wearers complete with dogtooth tweed jackets and the odd leather patch on the elbows, plus a dozen 4x4s and Land Rovers. We were each given a broom handle and piled into the trucks. The heifers had been spotted in a field about three miles away.

The fens are made up of deep, wide ditches called drains, usually with a high bank on either side, on top of which is a metalled road, farm track or drove road. On the other side you drop down into the fields.

We were on a drove road overlooking a field of potatoes, in the middle of which stood two heifers, one black and one white. After some weeks of dry sunny weather, there had been a thunderstorm the previous day and, due to the hard-baked ground, the water was sitting on the surface, giving the appearance of a paddy field.

Some twenty people then had the task of encircling the field which was enormous. Once everyone was in position, with a whistle blast accompaniment, the idea was that we were to close in and herd the heiffers towards a yard in one corner. Well, the white one started off on its own volition towards the yard, so we then had two groups of people, half of whom were now heading towards the black animal, which didn't look too happy.

As the men approached the beast, it decided to make a run for it, straight at me! Well, even from a hundred yards away it didn't look very little. There was a ton of animal splashing its way towards me at thirty miles an hour, and there I am with a broom handle at the ready. I rapidly decided this was no contest and, as I stepped to one side, the animal raced up the bank and straight past me down the other side, into a pond full of high rushes where it suddenly stopped and became ominously quiet.

So we had ten people surrounding the pond, and one brave soul went into the rushes with a stick to encourage it out. Crash! Out it came at a rate of knots, charging across a field and up a bank onto the main road, which brought all the traffic to a halt. Everyone clambered back into their trucks and the chase began.

By about midday, I had had enough and the farmer's wife wanted the beast shot as it was only a pet and worth about £10. It had already gone through two fences and was currently standing in the middle of a duck pond in a private garden.

I got a lift back to the farm and left John to his own devices. I returned to base and had a nice afternoon doing what I had planned to do in the morning.

John arrived back at about five o'clock. Putting a large map in front of me, he asked if I could find where the animals were now, as they had been moved to more secure accommodation. He sat down and watched as I did my map dowsing and found a spot left to right where my dowsing rod turned inwards. I then worked down the map until I got another reaction, at which point I made another mark – X marked the spot.

John immediately got up and telephoned someone. His opening remark was, "You'll never guess, but he's found them." Although the map covered several square miles, there was enough detail to mark buildings and the cross apparently went straight through the building where the heifers had been taken.

CHAPTER FIVE

Dowsing tunnels and ale

Our little London group had by now increased to about eight people and it seemed a good idea to have a day out somewhere. As a youngster, I had been brought up in a pub that had been built behind a fourteenth-century coaching inn. The inn had subsequently been demolished to form a car park and create a village square of sorts.

My dad had often told me there were three tunnels running in various directions from the old pub cellars. He had tried to walk or crawl through them but they had been in such a dangerous condition he had given up. Being young, I had not thought to ask where the tunnels were, but I knew one of the houses across the road had its own tunnel entrance in the cellar. All the houses were fourteenth- or fifteenth-century, so it would be interesting if we could dowse and find the outline of the cellars and trace the tunnels.

I wrote to all the house owners telling them what we were about, and what we would like to do. I asked if it was possible to visit their property if any of the tunnels went in their direction. All but one replied in the affirmative and on a sunny day we arrived to do our first group dowse.

We marked out the outline of the cellar and found the site of the old pub's well, and what was probably the steps down to the cellar. Our arrival had caused a lot of interest and the local residents invited us into their homes, as they were curious to see if we could unravel some of the mysteries and oddities for them. We had with us 'house detective' Roger Cockett, who asked if he could visit the lofts of the houses, as this is where most clues to the age of a building and any alterations that have been carried out are most evident. Having received permission, off he went with a torch.

We followed the line of the tunnel to where we knew the other entrance would be. It did not follow a straight line but formed a dogleg, which was a surprise. Another tunnel ran straight across the road and we were invited in by the owner to see where it led. It seemed that it ran into a cellar, but they didn't have a cellar. However, next door apparently did, and so did the building on the other side, so had theirs been covered over or filled in?

Strangely, the cellar only went halfway into the house, and was not to be found at the back. Enter our house detective all dusty from the loft. Explaining our 'findings' to him, he showed us that the house was originally half the depth and pointed out slots in the ceiling beam where the original wall had been. This made sense of the cellar going only half way back. He also said the three houses had originally been one, and had been divided up over the centuries.

We were also asked to find out where a garden water pipe ran from as the house was on a meter that did not move when the tap was turned full on. We followed the pipe to the next door garden, but this owner was the one who did not want us to visit, so we could not follow it any further. It also made sense that we only found one well and again it seemed to be in the garden of the out-of-bounds house. All very frustrating.

Our other tunnel went in another direction, headed for a garden, so again, the house owners let us run loose and we seemed to plot the outline of a pair of vaults which may have been for wine storage. If tunnels ran through the old cellar, no one would have been too interested in the ale but wines, spirits and possible contraband would have needed to be under lock and key. Unfortunately, the owner did not want us to investigate further and to this day there remains a question mark over this part.

Interestingly, the tunnel where we knew of the entrance had also in its long life belonged to a pub at one time, so was ale brewed in one cellar and trundled across to the other pub's cellar? We had an open invitation to visit the cellar of this house and the owners and the current pub landlord wanted us to visit them also, but we ran out of time. Today it is a domestic dwelling, but it had been an inn at one time, so there must have been three inns on top of each other at some time in the past. We had lots to look forward to. Little did we know!

This had been our first big trip out together and, thinking about it afterwards, we realised we had probably found what we were looking for but getting the proof was going to be a problem. If someone told me they thought I had vaults under my lawn, I would be curious to find out more, but in this case, the owner didn't want to know. Maybe he feared a loss in the value of his property. I would look at it the other way round. As for looking for the cellar that might be under his floor, we would have liked to have drilled a small hole through the next-door cellar wall, but the owner would not give us access or permission. More frustration!

The other point that came across was how different houses can be on the inside in terms of period, to how they appear on the outside, often having later fronts added on. I was starting to develop an interest in architecture and bricks which seemed to have a surprising variation through the ages.

Having our own house detective with us had brought things to light and helped make sense of our findings. Altogether it was a really good day and we looked forward to a return visit as other householders in the vicinity wanted us to visit them too.

Chapter Six

Watched or watched over?

Standing in a grassy field up on the North Downs, it was a glorious sunny day and I was working near the area of the Manor House which you have already read about. Just me and birdsong.

Working my way across the field with my dowsing rods, I was aware once more that someone was watching me. Looking to my left I could again see what looked like a window with a net curtain gently moving, and behind it, just visible in semi-darkness, was the appearance of the face that I have seen before. As I turned to get a better look at it, the vision disappeared and I was left looking at the landscape. I find this intriguing yet reassuring, but I don't know why.

Dowsing and marking out the line of an invisible wall, I was also aware of an elderly lady walking across the field with her dog. She had stopped and was watching me. I just carried on.

After a few minutes, an elderly man, also with dog, approached from the opposite side of the field and they met up in the middle. The lady started pointing at me and an animated conversation ensued. After a few more minutes, the lady approached saying the gentleman back there would like to know what I am doing. Unfortunately for her, the man started to walk away and the lady's cover was blown. I told her anyway and off she went, trying to catch up with the man.

It is amazing the number of times this happens. If I was in the middle of the desert, a dog walker would appear from behind a sand dune and want to know what I was doing. Most people I try and explain dowsing to seem totally unable to comprehend what a remarkable thing it is and where it could lead. Even more stunning is the fact that the longer a person has spent in academia, the less likely they are to show any interest. It's as if they are afraid of the subject, which they should not be, as it is something completely natural within us all.

* * * * *

The Renee Puddefoot demonstration of non-retinal vision had made quite an impact on me, and I had arranged for her to do the whole thing again with the London Group, which was by now just into double figures. We were then able to charge a membership fee which allowed us to offer payment to the speakers we hoped to attract. Our first visiting speaker was Renee and off she went with her story, with me acting as helper.

Once again out came the coloured papers, the letters of the alphabet, pages with a number on them and finally the simple pictures. One of our lady members – Rosie – was going great guns. She had identified all the coloured papers correctly and even described the shade of pink on one card.

She followed this up with all the alphabet letters and page numbers also correct. Everyone else were doing OK, getting between a third and a half right, which is impressive in itself, but Rosie was taking no prisoners. When we got to the two cards with pictures on, she got them right as well! Nine out of nine, that was brilliant and it was decided that a small prize was in order. In the following weeks we bought her a small map dowsing rod.

It is some years since I witnessed this tour-de-force, and more recently I read an article by some learnéd professor claiming that non-retinal vision was impossible. Well, I've got news for him. It is possible. I've done quite well at it myself and how does he explain Rosie getting nine cards out of nine right?

Our little group was a talented bunch. We had a multi-media artist, one or two others who designed and made trinkets of one sort or another, a cross-channel swimmer, someone who could see auras and Guy, who had learnt to dowse as a child. He also had the ability to carry out hypnosis and do regressions and he offered to regress a member of the group if they were willing.

We had two volunteers and at the end of one meeting, I asked those who did not want to witness it to leave. Personally, I thought it a bit creepy and would leave with who ever else wanted to go. Nobody moved, they were all up for it, so as chairman, I couldn't set a bad example by leaving on my own, and decided to grin and bear it.

Our first volunteer, Alan, sat down in a comfortable chair and Guy began his hypnosis. I could feel myself 'going' as well, and had to play around with a set of keys to keep awake. It was all a bit of an anticlimax, as Alan was on a beach somewhere with next to nothing on and no sign of anyone or anything.

Despite Guy moving him around the landscape, he seemed to be on an island with no sense of time period, so he was 'brought back'. Interestingly, when he came to, he said he felt as though he had been on holiday and could he go back because it was cheap!

It was too late after that for our second volunteer to go in the chair and we had to hold it over for the next meeting.

Another of our home-grown speakers is Ced Jackson, who gave our Group a talk on the subject of *Sacred Geometry*. It was all new to me, so I and many others did not know what to expect, but he arrived armed with protractors and sheets of plain paper. We had to draw a circle and then mark it off using the same spacing. From there, just arcing across the circle we ended up with the Christian 'fish' symbol and with another arc, a bishop's mitre and so it went on.

This introduction to the subject made a big impact on me and I recently bought a book called *Sacred Geometry* by Stephen Skinner which should be in every maths teacher's armoury as it shows how mathematics and geometry are in everything around us, from the pattern of petals on a flower to music and architecture, which explains why the human eye likes certain shapes but not others.

Finally, while boasting about our membership, one of our London members can see auras and, as he is a very down-to-earth person, I have no reason to doubt him. Apparently he has always seen them just as clearly as we see the nose on someone's face, and had assumed everyone else saw them too. It was only when he was in his twenties that he began to realise maybe he was fairly unique.

He is also good at psychometry, holding an object and getting details of the history of the people who have been in contact with it. This is a subject on its own, but something most dowsers should try. It can throw up up some interesting 'visions'.

Chapter Seven

Lest we forget – Remanence

Shortly after this we went on our second trip to where my Dad's old pub had been. We had arranged to visit the house where we knew one of the tunnels led. On entering, the interior took on a totally different aspect from the outside, which we were told was a nineteenth-century makeover. The inside was fifteenth century and quite stunning.

This made some sense for there being a tunnel. We were told that the house we were in was originally just part of a much larger house that, over the centuries, had been divided up into smaller dwellings. So as not to give too much away, the owners of the other parts of the original house would be pleased if we investigated them as well. This was music to our ears.

Visiting the cellar of the first house, we saw the closed-off entrance to the tunnel we had followed from across the road. The original cellar wall had been breached and on dowsing the cellar, we seemed to find a well beneath the stone flags. Going back upstairs, I started to dowse the outline of the cellar through the floor and it followed the shape of the existing cellar except at one point.

By a process of elimination it seemed to be the original steps down to the cellar before the wall had been breached. This also made sense. The owners were fascinated and gave us a guided tour of the house and garden.

At this point, we asked if we could go over the garden as well and Alan Hayday and I began to investigate. We soon picked up a drainage channel and then noticed how obvious it was as the grass was a slightly different colour.

Along the back of the small garden we seemed to pick up the foundations of a seemingly sturdy structure with walls about one metre wide, with small rooms. When we started looking for windows, very few showed up. We felt this could have been a place to keep precious goods and articles secure.

At this point I should add that when dowsing for underground foundations, we can pick up where windows and doors used to be although if you dug down to the foundations, those details would not be visible.

We pick up a 'remanence' of such details and it helps us to understand what the building had been used for. This may be a difficult concept to take in, but that is how it works.

We tried to date the foundations and found ourselves in the fourteenth century. There seemed to be a tie-in with the Knights Templar but it was a bit late for them, as they had been disbanded in the fourteenth century. However, if that is what it dowses, then I am inclined to go with it.

The foundations followed into the next garden and we had permission to investigate further. Unfortunately there was a big rockery in the way and we could not clamber over that, so our investigation ended.

The owners of this house had to go out, but they said we were welcome to come back another day. Then the people across the road wanted us to see if we could find a well that was mentioned in their deeds.

The building across the road had also been a pub, and was next door to where my Dad's pub had been. I remembered it as a pub when I lived there. It was now a private residence and we were welcomed by the owners and shown a large gravel yard to the rear of the premises. Could we find a well?

Alan and I started on our search and soon found the likely spot. The owner then found a scaffolding pole and tried pushing it into the ground. It didn't go far, but he was keen to investigate further when he had the time. This was music to our ears too. We marked the spot on a simple plan and having done enough for that day, retired to a local hostelry.

CHAPTER EIGHT

Dowsing for Second World War aircraft

I have found that dowsing can be extremely tiring. It requires a relaxed concentration while you are posing questions in such a way as to be totally unambiguous, because the quality of the question is paramount if you want to obtain the true answer. We get things wrong when our questioning is suspect. It's like a computer, garbage in, garbage out.

After about two hours you get the feeling that your brain is turning to jelly and then it is time to stop because any dowsing done in those circumstances becomes a nonsense. The correct information is always to hand; it is down to us to interpret it correctly. Unfortunately there are people about who think they can dowse but can't, and they foul things up for the rest of us.

I was approached by someone involved with the Second World War aircraft salvage team who hunt out the sites of aircraft that crashed during the war. Apparently, they had used a dowser on another expedition with some success, so could I help them with a site close to the junction of what is now the M25 and the A2 in Kent. On meeting with some of the members at the Second World War museum at Shoreham, Kent, I was given a map of the area and told that an eye witness had seen a plane crash in the vicinity.

My first action was to take the map home and map dowse it, taking a wider area than that suggested. I couldn't pick up any sign of a crash site in the fields mentioned but some way off, by a couple of remote cottages, I seemed to get a signal. This was nowhere near where the eye witness said it was, but that was a long time ago and the landscape changes, which does not help. However, small pieces of aluminium had been found, so I may have been having an off day.

I reported my findings and asked Alan Hayday if he would like to help out, which he was happy to do, so a day was set to visit the fields in question with a research team. We were on rolling chalk downland with a thin top-covering of soil and poor grass, well nibbled by horses, so we set off crossing the field looking for a reaction to a crashed aircraft from our rods. After a while, we seemed to be homing in on two sites, not one, which were about 70 feet apart.

Alan felt that an aircraft engine was central to one site and about 15 feet down. Had the plane hit the ground with secondary material bouncing off the hard surface and coming to grief at a spot further away? We scoured the ground looking for any scraps of man-made material but without success.

The centres of the two sites were spray marked, the plan being to get a mechanical digger in to open up a trench at a later date. Due to work commitments, neither of us could be on site when the digger arrived, but we heard afterwards the ground was so hard, every time the bucket was put down, the body of the digger started to lift up, so that put paid to that exercise.

I am not aware that any further attempts were made to investigate the site, but my feeling was that we had come unstuck because our dowsing ability had been clouded by someone putting into our heads the thought that a crash had happened there and we therefore felt almost honour bound to come up with something.

This is something else to learn. Never ask for prior information about a site. Go to it with a blank mind and start from scratch every time. People try to help by saying that there used to be something here or there and, in truth, it is often hearsay with the spot they point to being wrong anyway. So a word of advice, be true to your own dowsing and ignore all other (mis)information. This was the one thing we learnt from this venture and it has held us in good stead ever since.

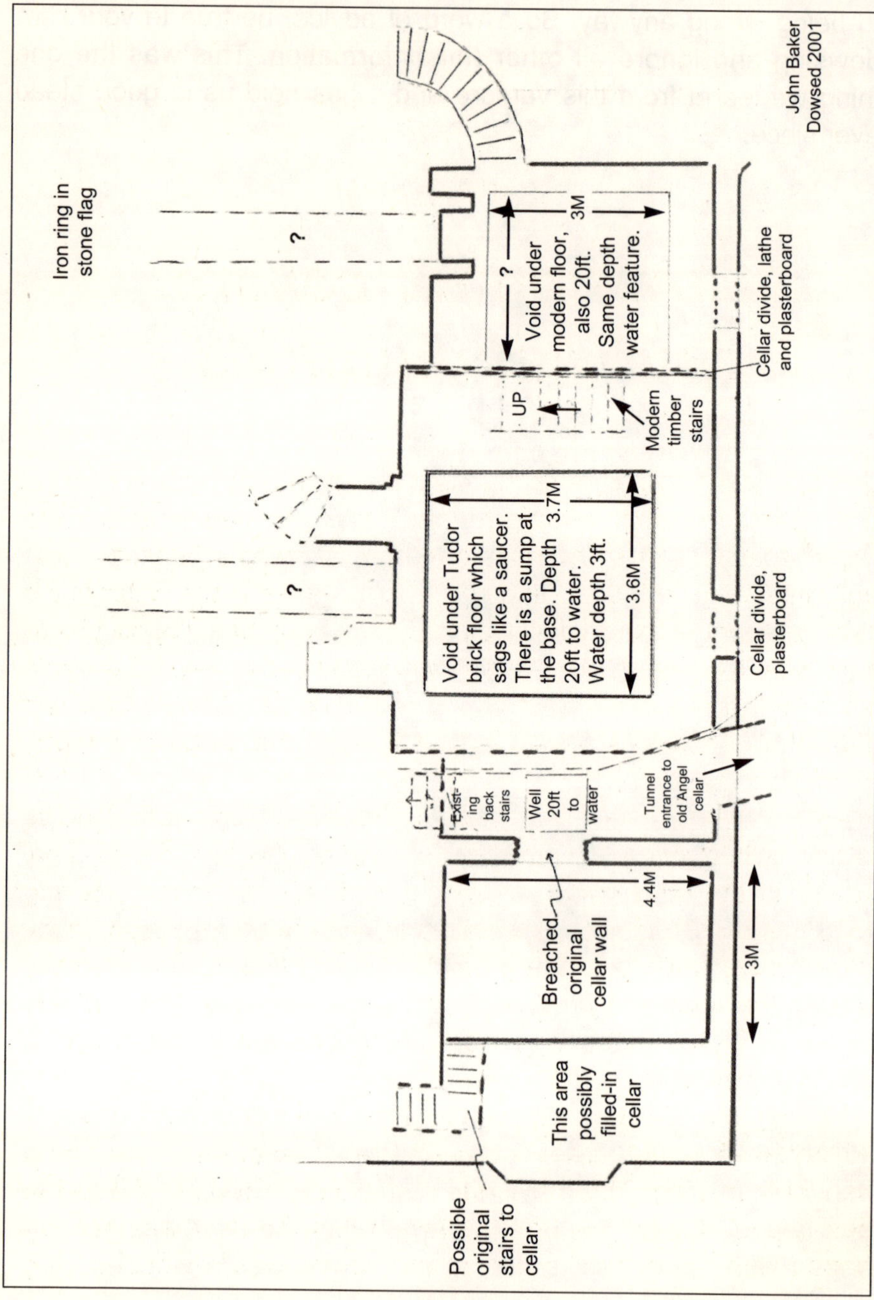
John Baker
Dowsed 2001
Iron ring in
stone flag
?
Void under
modern floor,
also 20ft.
Same depth
water feature.
3M
?
Cellar divide, lathe
and plasterboard
UP
Modern
timber
stairs
Void under Tudor
brick floor which
sags like a saucer.
There is a sump at
the base. Depth
20ft to water.
Water depth 3ft.
3.7M
3.6M
?
Cellar divide,
plasterboard
Exist-
ing
back
stairs
Well
20ft
to
water
Tunnel
entrance to
old Angel
cellar
4.4M
Breached
original
cellar wall
3M
This area
possibly
filled-in
cellar
Possible
original
stairs to
cellar

Chapter Nine

Dowsing for cellars, pubs and tunnels

On going to my dad's old pub for a third time, on my own on this occasion, I was given access by the people across the road to further investigate the group of three houses. I was really interested in the existing cellars and started in the cellar of the first house where the original wall had been breached. I'm curious to know what is under the cellars and in the first passageway I seem to find a well going down about thirty feet to water. I know from old plans that the village well was just outside the building, so why another one so close?

As I dowsed, I had a big sketchpad on which I jotted down details. While in the cellar area, I wondered where the original access to the cellar was before the wall was breached. Moving along the walls, I found what seems to have been the steps down. At this point, I go up to the ground floor and look for the stairway through the floor and up it pops, a narrow stairway with a ninety degree bend in it that brings it up on the side-wall of the house. A sensible place to put it.

Moving into the next house, there were wooden steps down to the cellar that had been converted into a dining room with chandelier lighting. The table was supported on pieces of wood to keep it level. Closer inspection showed that the floor was saucer-shaped with Tudor bricks and at the centre was a wooden plug

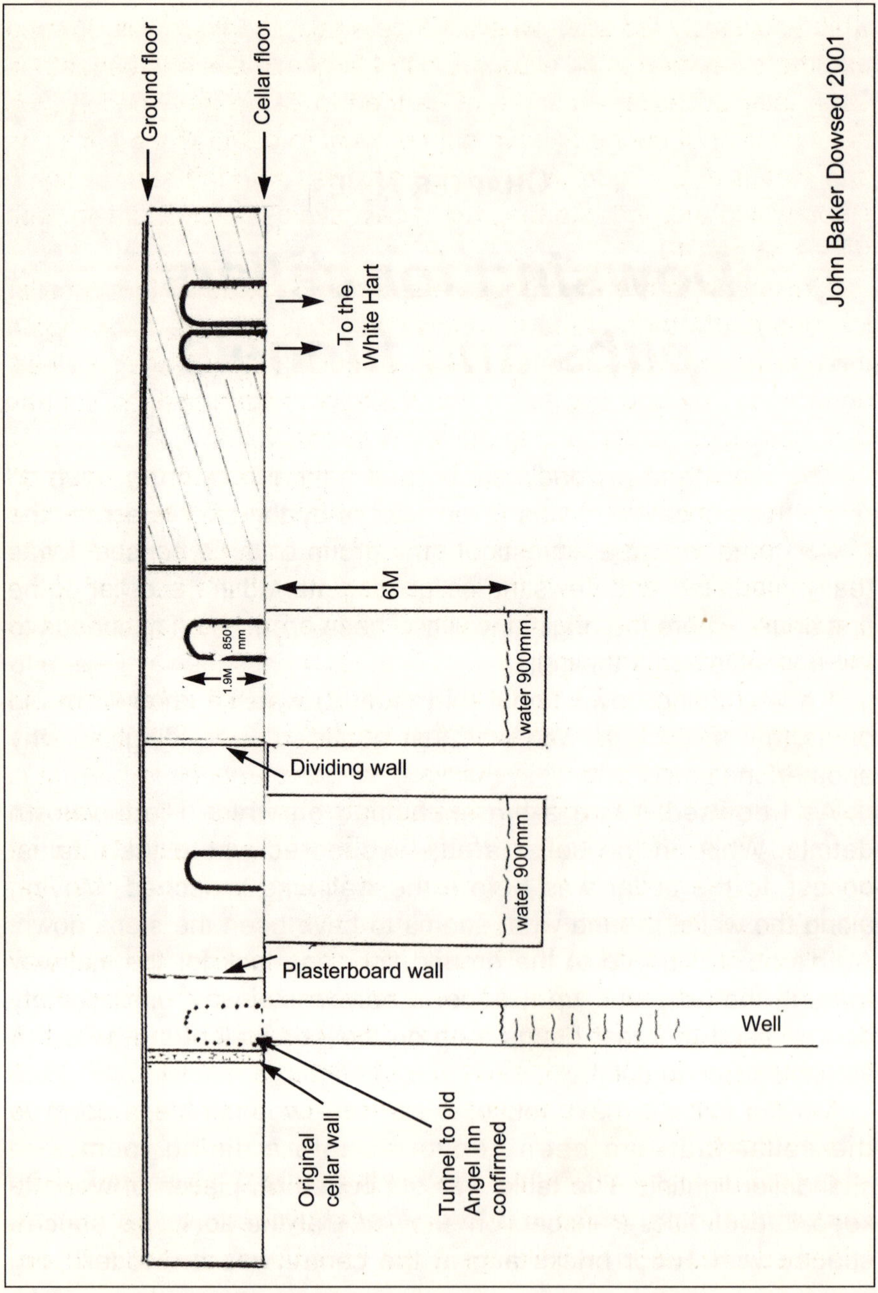
Ground floor
Cellar floor
John Baker Dowsed 2001
To the
White Hart
6M
.850
mm
1.9M
water 900mm
Dividing wall
water 900mm
Plasterboard wall
Well
Original
cellar wall
Tunnel to old
Angel Inn
confirmed

which obviously led somewhere. Once again, the floor was dowsed and there seemed to be a square pit of large dimensions beneath it. On a later occasion a couple of us tried to lift up the wooden plug but it would not budge and we did not want to damage the bricks. In one corner of the room was a brick archway with the start of some steps which merged into the wall. Again sketches were drawn, see pages 38 and 40.

Moving on to the third house and again back down to the cellar by means of stone steps this time, we have a stone floor. Again there is an archway set in the inner wall but it does not seem to lead anywhere. Dowsing the floor I find a similar square-shaped void as in the previous house, and to the same depth.

Looking at the archway again, and having previously been all over the ground floor, it seems to line up with a stone flag at the rear of the house with the remains of an iron ring in it. Going back up to the ground floor and dowsing the passageway, there seemed to be a shallow void under the floor which stopped at the flagstone with the ring. All most intriguing.

I wanted to find out if there was another separate cellar which no one knew about. The owner of the house told me that the large hallway area was originally the yard where carriages would have pulled up and I went over this area but found nothing. There was still another ground-floor room to check and as I walked towards the far end of it, I seemed to hit another void, but only about three feet across. Was this a tunnel?

I went to the rear of the house and, starting from the end wall I did find a void, but it did not line up with the one in the front room. So I went back to the front room and walked its length again, this time finding a double void, each one about three feet wide. So back to the rear of the building and yes, it carried on under the building as a twin tunnel.

On the opposite side of the road at this point is another fifteenth-century building which until very recently used to be an inn. I seemed to have three buildings which in centuries past all sold ale, two were coaching inns and the third a tavern, all three seemingly connected by tunnels. Further investigation was called for.

I contacted a brewery and asked one of their experts what the procedure was for brewing beer in the fifteenth and sixteenth centuries. I was told that in those days hops were not used, it was just water and malted barley, heated up together in seething pits. This produced ale, not beer as we know it today, and ale did not travel well or keep for very long. You brewed it and drank it.

So was this layout of a well and the two large pits where the ale was brewed for all three inns, and did the tunnels allow the ale to be moved quickly and easily from site to site? As an added bonus, these tunnels could have been used for smuggling contraband and also as escape routes for anyone suffering religious persecution.

A couple of years later I heard from the owner of the building where the twin tunnels seemed to be heading. He had met an elderly lady who said that as a child she had played in the cellar tunnels! It is so frustrating to get this sort of information and not be able to find out more, at least up to the time of writing.

Chapter Ten

Lessons Learned

I had been asked by an acquaintance, Dennis Molyneux, if I would visit a field recently handed over to his village by a building company. His committee wanted to know if there might be anything of interest buried in the field. Oh, and could I also teach interested members to dowse. Being up for anything I said yes and did a quick visit to the field before the organised trip.

Prior to the day, Dennis was going to bury a piece of pipe in the field as something to look for. He phoned me and explained that as I walked through a gap in the hedge, a short way along on my left is a pyracantha bush. "The piece of pipe is buried there," he said.

On the appointed day I arrived at the car park near the field to find a large crowd milling about. We had picked the same day as the local archery group, so we had one group of people with bows and arrows and another group with metal coat hangers waiting for Dennis to cut them down into dowsing rods. The archers were saying, "You can't fire an arrow with coat hangers", and the dowsing group were saying, "You can't dowse with a bow". Superficially, both items have the same shape.

I went through the gap in the hedge and found the pyracantha bush. There in front of it, and rather too close to the bush, was a scuffed piece of grass. The first members of the group were coming through the hedge and I was getting them to walk towards the hedge to try dowsing for the metal pipe. Mysteriously, as they passed over where they should have got a reaction, nothing happened. On top of that, they were getting caught up in the vicious prickles of the hedge. It seemed a daft spot to pick. The main problem was that nobody was getting any reaction. Usually someone does. With the last of the committee in the field, Dennis appeared and asked why I had got everyone at that spot because that was not where the pipe was buried!

I had to point out that this was the first pyracantha bush in the hedge which is where he said he would bury the pipe, and there was the bare earth in the grass where he had buried it. “Oh,” he said, “I missed that bush, it’s further along.” No wonder nothing was found. So we had another go at the ‘proper’ site and having been caught once, I checked to see if it was there and got a reaction, but everyone else was struggling.

Having been given a plan of the field prior to the visit, I had map dowsed an interesting spot which looked to be part of a wall. On site it was at the top of the slope so we walked to where I thought we might discover something, and asked for assistance with measuring tapes and for someone to draw a plan of what was starting to appear. A very smart lady in twin set and pearls offered to draw and write down the measurements and, once I’d explained how to do it, off we went.

The structure seemed to be of Norman origin, the first time I had encountered anything of this period. One or two members of the group were also starting to get reactions with their rods and this always generates a sense of excitement. With marker sticks placed in the ground, a nice line about a metre thick started to show, then it turned, creating a corner, and went across the field until we got to the boundary where private gardens began. So that was as far as we could go. With people measuring and the lady drawing and writing everything down, things looked good and everyone seemed pleased, so we started to pack up and remove the marker sticks.

The lady doing the drawing then handed back the drawing pad. All that was on it was a series of squiggles and dimensions scribbled all over the place. It was a mess, but what could I say?

I pointed it out to Dennis and he apologised, saying that the lady had good and bad days but she volunteered so quickly, he couldn't do much about it. So the whole exercise was a waste of time.

This event taught me two valuable lessons. Firstly to trust no one but myself and secondly, to check early on if people were doing things right. It also confirmed that bows used in archery do not make good dowsing rods.

Chapter Eleven

Self hypnosis or self delusion?

Our London Group was slowly expanding and by popular demand, Renee Puddefoot was invited back to talk to us, this time on relaxation and self hypnosis techniques. We had now discovered that Renee was the Ladies Over 60s World High Diving Champion and for her age, remarkably fit. Being of the old school, firm but fair, we told new members they would have to stay behind and do lines if they were late for this demonstration.

As usual the talk was fascinating. Attempting self hypnosis for the first time, we all went under to some degree but not enough to become unaware of our surroundings.

It seemed to me that if I could incorporate this teaching when I next gave a talk, getting people relaxed would increase their chances of success when they tried dowsing for themselves.

I did not have long to wait. A few weeks later I was asked to give a talk and demonstration to a University of the Third Age (U3A) group in Essex. I was sent a map of my destination and its immediate surroundings, an old village school with the church next door. I dowsed the map and there seemed to be the remains of a building in the church grounds, so I decided it would be a talk and then a walk next door to do some practical work.

The day was hot and sunny. I was met at the school by various people, mainly retired folk, a few ladies who lunched and a peppery old Colonel who stated in a voice that could be heard two counties away, "I have to say I view the whole thing with scepticism but welcome anyway."

I gave my talk to about twenty people and decided to put my new relaxation technique to work, getting them to unwind. I asked them all to close their eyes, which everyone did except the Colonel, who I had to encourage a second time to close his.

I then took them on a little mind journey and at one point I asked them all to put out their hands to touch something. I got the shock of my life when everyone physically stretched out their arms. What had I done? Had I really hypnotised them? More importantly, could I get them back?

A cold sweat broke out as I considered my options. They all had their eyes shut; I could sneak out, hop in the car and make a run for it. I decided to carry on with the journey and got everyone to a point where I asked them to come back to the hall in their own time, and open their eyes.

Gradually eyes opened, but it took a good few seconds for some of them, and boy, was I relieved once everyone was awake again. I decided some fresh air was in order so off we went to the church next door.

It wasn't long before almost all of them were getting their rods to move at a point where, according to my map, there should have been a buried wall. As you will know by now, the first time the rods respond to you is a real thrill and quite elating. Even the Colonel was starting to see something happen.

All too soon we returned to the school hall and, after refreshments I showed them how to create a ley line, find it and then get rid of it again, which we must always do. This was the highlight of the visit and at the end the old Colonel came up to me, shook my hand and said, "I won't be able to sleep tonight." Mission accomplished!

As a rider to this story, two of the U3A members joined the London Group and went on to do sterling work with archaeologists in Maldon, Essex and another site in the county. I had discovered that my relaxation technique could have some surprises in store for me. Next time I would be prepared, and over all I was pleased that so many people had a response.

Chapter Twelve

Courage and Confidence

Remembering Guy and his experiences in the Royal Marines, I contacted the Royal Engineers at Chatham to see whether they still used dowsing techniques. I was especially interested because it was members of the RE who formed the BSD in 1933 in order to carry on with dowsing when they left the army.

I was invited to visit their library in Chatham and was told that the librarian would look up some references for me. Brompton Barracks is an extremely impressive group of Victorian buildings, each one set in its own grounds. The entrance to the library is down a wide flight of steps and the whole place opens up in front of you, a bit like the old British Library.

I followed up my visit with a letter of thanks, which the Royal Engineers published in their Journal because I had also asked if anyone else had any dowsing experiences to report. I received some interesting replies which covered adventures in India to dowsing in Northern Ireland. Incidents seemed to dwindle by the 1960s, probably with the advent of computers and expensive electronic equipment. I feel this is a pity because the best computers in the world are between our ears. We just have to learn how to use them.

At about this time the BSD was offering a tutor training course in Lincoln and I decided it would be in my best interests to attend as I

FAWKHAM & ASH ARCHAEOLOGICAL GROUP

Excavations Director: Roger A C Cockett
Address:
Phone:
Email:

To: John Baker Esq
68 Ironmill Lane
Crayford
Kent
DA1 4RR

19 June 2005

Dear John

WORK AT THE SITE OF FAWKHAM MEDIEVAL MANOR IN 2004/2005

This note is to record my gratitude for the dowsing work which you carried out in the early Spring of 2004 at Fawkham Manor, when I asked you to explore the area south of the pebbled yard area extending south from "Building C".

You will recall that you found a wall running east-west some 5 metres beyond our excavated area. Subsequently last year we based our excavation strategy on your results and we duly found the wall, though it had been almost entirely robbed away.

We have continued in this vicinity in 2005 and your assistance has helped us make sense of this part of the manorial complex. The Archaeological Group and I are extremely grateful to you for pointing us in the right direction.

Yours sincerely

Roger

ROGER A C COCKETT

enjoyed passing on to other interested parties what little I had learnt. The course was over a weekend and our base was on Cathedral property. It was OK but a bit austere. There were six or eight of us being tutored on how to put over the subject and what checks to put in to ensure everyone was keeping up. The workshops went on late and dinner was even later, leaving just time for a quick trip to the pub to relax. The problem for me with eating late is that my feet get very hot in bed! I usually have to stick them out from under the covers which is what I did that night.

The following day we worked hard, with myself and fellow-trainee Shaun Ogborne being asked to produce a programme to teach archaeological dowsing. Again it was a late finish, an even later dinner and another quick trip to the pub. One of the girls on the course was known to be a bit psychic and suddenly said that the previous night, someone or something had tried to pull her out of bed by her foot.

This was something I didn't want to know and on retiring later, decided that no matter how hot my feet became, I was not sticking them out of bed. So there I lay, moving them from one cool part of the bed to another and generally spending a sleepless night.

I was glad to leave Lincoln. With this course under my belt, I had the opportunity to go on the BSD professional register. In order to be included I had to have three independent confirmations that I had dowsed a given site and that subsequent investigation had proved me correct. Letters explaining what I had done had to be sent to the BSD, who then obtained further confirmation by contacting the people concerned.

With archaeology, it takes a long time. It is easy for me to go over a field and say so-and-so is there, but for a dig to start sometimes takes years. However, I have been lucky and had more than the required three finds and the people I had done work for were happy to confirm the details. I was then put on the professional dowsers list for archaeology. To qualify to be on the list for water divining was just one find away.

Dartford District Archaeological Group

Director: Christopher Baker

Affiliated to the Council for British Archaeology, Kent Archaeological Society and Dartford Arts Council

Please reply to:

Chris Baker
C/O Dartford Borough Museum

Dartford
Kent

The General Secretary
The British Society of Dowsers
Sycamore Barn
Hastingleigh
Ashford
Kent
TN25 5HW

Tel

6 October 2003

Dear Sir

Mr John Baker

I am writing to you with regard to the above named member who joined the Group in June 1996.

Since this time John has dowsed on many occasions at our excavations, locating features some of which were later proven by excavation.

Yours faithfully

Chris Baker

Chris Baker
Director
Dartford District Archaeological Group

Registered Charity No. 1056142

Having come to know a few more people higher up in the BSD, I thought it a good idea to go to another annual Congress, this time in Cirencester. It would be a weekend of lectures, workshops, literature to buy, and would give me a chance to dip into other aspects of dowsing such as earth energies, healing and to some extent, water. There was nothing on archaeology which in a way suited me.

It was to be held at the Agricultural College and was my first visit to Cirencester. The College was an imposing building with high ceilings and wide staircases. On the Friday evening there was a drinks get together and I knew just two people in a gathering of some 180 or so attendees.

So it was a matter of throwing yourself in, saying who you were and where you came from, and hope no one was going to be stand-offish. There were no worries on that score. I have discovered that the one thing dowsers are good at is talking, and if you're a good listener, you are in your element. A welcoming address by the President and dinner with wine finished off a pleasant evening.

The next two days were a whirlwind of talks and workshops. I made a number of contacts with people who would be prepared to come and talk to our London Group. I sat in on lectures on water divining, healing and earth energies, the latter seeming less off the wall than I had previously thought.

The water divining showed me I was on the right track and I was impressed with the healing aspect. With healing, it should be pointed out that it can be an aid to recovery, not a substitute for visiting a GP or surgery. And dowsers are not allowed to claim they can diagnose anything. Only qualified members of the medical profession are allowed to diagnose.

I was particularly keen to attend the workshops on healing. I had a neighbour who had neck and head problems with almost continual headaches and she had said that I could practise healing on her. So far I had resisted the urge. After all this was a person under medication, not some inanimate object. That said, I was very tempted to try it to see if I could bring about any improvement.

Michael McMahon

John Baker
68 Iron Mill Lane
Crayford
Kent
DA1 4RR
01322 525975

15 June 2004

Dear John,

Just a short note to thank you for the work you carried out to my back as you know I came to you quite desperate after seeing so many Chiropractors, Osteopaths, Physiotherapists and even an Acupuncturist. I was extremely sceptical considering you were not even going to lay a hand on my back but desperate does what desperate needs. At the time I didn't think anything had worked and came out the same as I went in. The next couple of days there was an improvement and by the end of the week I was walking upright again without all the discomfort I had for months before.

I know I have called to thank you but I just wanted to write to you and thank you again.

Kind Regards

Michael McMahon

My mentor, Dan Wilson, had come to my house on a few occasions when I had found someone who was wiling to try anything. One lady brought to my house was bent over with back pain. The friend who brought her said it was the first time she had been out of bed for a week. I felt quite embarrassed when I helped the poor sufferer into my living room, leaving her with Dan.

Her friend and I sat in another room and waited. About half an hour later the session was over and she was helped back to the car. It was important to Dan and me to hear whether there was any improvement or otherwise, so we asked them to let us know.

Two days later we were informed that the evening after her visit, she suddenly decided she wanted to go to Bluewater shopping centre and despite her husband's misgivings, off they went. On returning to the car it started to rain and this woman, who had previously been bent over with genuine pain, was suddenly running to the car with a bag full of shopping. Everyone was amazed and to this day I still am.

This and other events made me even more curious to see if I could do healing by dowsing and I eventually decided I would take up my neighbour's offer if she was still happy about it and up for the experiment. She said she was, so I started my first healing session. I can't explain what I did because I don't know myself. All I can say is that it is about concentrating on opening up blocked channels and for whatever reason, it often works. To this day, I have never been visited again by sciatica since my first experience of healing with Dan Wilson, so even if it is the placebo effect, if it works, does it matter how?

The next day I asked my neighbour how she was and she said that the headache had gone. She was keen to repeat the exercise a few days later. Over the next few weeks, the healing seemed to get rid of the headaches for a while but they gradually came back. In all fairness, she had quite a serious condition and I was a complete novice, but there was some pain relief and I've since discovered that healing by dowsing can be quite effective in the head and neck area.

You can dowse to see if someone else has a health problem but you can't dowse your own body because you have a vested interest in not wanting any problem to show up. One dowser I know enjoys a drink, but he has a medical condition which is made worse by too much alcohol. So when he's in a pub and unsure whether he can have another or not, he asks his pendulum whether it is all right to go ahead.

And of course, the pendulum always answers in a positive manner because the man himself wants another drink!

CHAPTER THIRTEEN

A Scilly Idea

One day I had a phone call from a farmer asking me if I knew anything about pentagons and their effect on crop growth. I had heard nothing about it before so he offered to send me some photocopied information to see if I could help in any way, and to telephone him when I had read it.

The information soon arrived. It was photocopied from a book written by a Scilly Isles farmer, a Mr Tabraham. It was titled *Solar Energy and Dowsing in the Isles of Scilly** and went back to the days before industrial glasshouses and produce being flown around the world. In those days, the Scillies grew an early spring flowering *Soleil d'or narcissi* and the earlier these flowers came to the London market, the greater the premium the farmer would receive. If you got flowers to market before Christmas, you had hit the jackpot. Many odd ideas were tried to encourage early flowering.

The book gives a three-year documented history of how, by dowsing a field or area in the shape of a pentagon, bulbs would flower sooner than in using any other method. The idea was that the pentagon is created with the intent that within it the ground temperature would rise. Charts in the book seemed to prove this. The outcome of early growing was more money in the bank, and dowsing pentagons was carried out with some zeal.

The farmer who sent the photocopied details to me, Richard, was interested to see whether I and other dowsers could re-create this

**Available from the BSD*

ground warming effect on his farm. His idea was that a field of pick-your-own strawberries could be planted and, with his strawberries ripening quicker than those on adjacent farms, he would get a better price for his crop.

This was fascinating stuff and I was keen to give it a go. According to Mr Tabraham, one of the peculiarities of all this was that the effect of the warming gradually moved south.

We had to wait for land on the farm to be cleared and the farmer decided to plant borage, a fast growing crop, so we would soon get an answer. We also had to find some ground thermometers in order to register temperature variations. There was one restriction in that no metal object could be placed within the pentagon; if metal did go inside the area, the warming effect could be lost. Since thermometers usually have at least some metal parts, this needed further research.

Chapter Fourteen

Seeking a new home

While all that was going on, the London and Thamesside Dowsers suddenly had a new problem. Guy and Leisbett who let us use their house for our meetings were planning to emigrate, which meant we would have to find a new venue in the same area, as everyone now knew their way to Mile End.

Our numbers had grown to about 15 by then, and if they all turned up for a meeting, it was a tight squeeze. We were sad to have to say goodbye, not just to Guy and Leisbett, but to the endless cups of coffee, tea and biscuits. Worst of all, we might have to pay for a new meeting place. With very limited funds, this was bad news indeed.

Before our next meeting, I wandered around Mile End looking for a suitable venue, ideally a room over a pub, but the first pubs I visited didn't have anything to offer. A church hall was too big and anyway, it was needed for other groups on a weekend. Finally, two streets away I discovered the Coborn Arms, where we could have use of the darts room free of charge. The landlord said he hoped to get money in from drinks and pub lunches, so it seemed to be an ideal solution all round. There was also much more room for our members and we had the space for slide shows and speakers. We could also get a website up and running which would give us the chance to draw in more members.

Our last meeting at Guy's was a bit sad as, without the use of his house, we would not have had such a pleasant base. We said goodbye to Guy and family who were off to New Zealand. It was pastures new for all of us.

The next London Dowsers meeting was our first at the Coborn Arms and about a dozen members turned up. In a room which would have easily held thirty plus people, for the first time we had room to breathe. Our speaker was BSD member David Dixon, who had been working with water diviners in Guyana, South America, where it rains non-stop for three months, then nothing for nine months. As Guyana is nearly all rock, the water just runs off the surface and there is nothing left other than in a few gulleys.

David and a few other diviners had been working in the hills trying to get boreholes into the rock but the drills wore out quickly and, being costly items, progress had been disappointing. There was some success but these problems brought home to us how much we take water for granted. No flushing toilets, no showers, no baths and no fresh drinking water except from a government bowser which imposes a charge on people who are dirt-poor and have to wash their clothes in muddy ponds. Yet in the photographs David brought to show us, everyone looked so clean. It always amazes me how these people manage it.

The new pub venue seemed popular with everyone and with food available, after our meeting was over, a number stayed behind to indulge and things seemed to be more sociable. In fact, although our meeting finished at one o'clock, I was still there at 2.30 pm. As I have said before, dowsers can talk.

CHAPTER FIFTEEN

The Pentagon Effect

At last Richard, our farmer wanting to try the pentagon effect, said his field was ready for me. I took along two fellow dowsers, Vicky and Alan.

The farmhouse was a mix of fourteenth- to eighteenth-century buildings and interesting in its own right, but we were met by Richard who took us to a nice sloping field full of clover with no tree cover, which meant the ground had equal exposure to the sun throughout the day.

A 20 foot by 15 foot area was measured off and, having been told the effect moves south, we decided that the point of the pentagon should face north. All three of us walked through the area with our dowsing rods prior to putting in wooden stakes. We had no reaction from anything in the ground which seemed to be clear of any anomalies.

In went the stakes and, starting at one corner and working anti-clockwise, I touched the first stake and then proceeded to walk around the perimeter of the pentagon with the intent that the ground inside the area would become warmer than elsewhere. Having walked round once I noticed that the single rod I was holding turned slightly inward towards the pentagon.

On my second circuit, it had turned in a little more and by the time I had done five circuits, the rod was pointing across my body. I decided this was the job completed, as this is the found position when dowsing. We all walked through the newly-formed pentagon and as we entered its inner space, our rods crossed and remained so until we left the other side. Clearly, something had happened.

We had with us a couple of earth thermometers, both made with some metal components but we hoped not enough to upset the system. One was placed within the pentagon and one outside it to see if we could measure any temperature variations. It was now down to the farmer to check the thermometers each day, and also once a week dowse the pentagon to top up the charge.

At this point we left the field to get some refreshments and a little later returned to see if there had been any change in the thermometers. There was a two degree difference with the inner one showing the increase. This was quite amazing and we left in high spirits, with the farmer agreeing to follow up and let us know what happened over the next few weeks.

Before leaving I was given a plan of the farm to map dowse as a Roman road went through the land, which had been proven by a dig, so perhaps there were other things in the vicinity.

CHAPTER SIXTEEN

Mind Games

I had received a phone call from someone in Cambridge asking if I would be interested in going to a remote viewing exercise. Now this is not going to some windswept mountain and looking at the view; it is something the American CIA had been working on for some time and it was used in Vietnam.

The idea is that the human mind can travel outside the physical frame and, with guidance, can home in on someone or something previously unknown, in another country, or next door. It is a bit like dowsing in a way.

I had seen something on television about it where those involved in the experiments began having mental problems after some time, and the programme was consequently wound down, although it may well still be running somewhere. In fact, I'm sure it is, but in a slightly different form.

I'll have a go at most things and ended up in a basement in central London with six or seven others and our two-man instruction team, all seated round a large table in the middle of which was a pile of brown envelopes. One envelope was selected and we were told it had a picture inside it. Without seeing it, we were asked to visualise what the picture was of. We had to find out where the picture was taken, describe any view or people we could 'see', pick up on any sounds, and taste if there was something edible. In other words, we had to use our five senses if the picture demanded it. There was a start and finish protocol to observe and that was it.

Closing my eyes I soon homed in on a scene where I was overlooking but close to a small Spanish-style church, all white with a bell tower and bell exposed. It was on a hot, dry headland and below it there was a beach and blue sea with little breeze. The air was filled with the scent of pine trees. That was my picture and when we had all made the necessary notes we were asked one by one to tell the others what we had 'seen'.

The first person started by saying they had pictured a white church. This surprised me. I was even more surprised when the scene I had pictured was described by someone else. Everything in my scene, this person was explaining. The same with the next person and by the time it was my turn, I had nothing to add except that everyone else had already covered what I had 'seen'. This was amazing, we all had the same mental picture and now it was time to open the envelope. Out slipped an A4 colour print of an American Cadillac with four people in it, going up a steep road at an angle of about 30º, with a background of trees. Nothing like our remote view!

Someone in the group had controlled our thought processes so that we all got the same picture. That is what we were told and having met so many people with unusual abilities, I would not put it beyond the realms of possibility. Neither would I take it on board as totally acceptable. It seemed to me that dowsing was a better way to get information because visualisation does come into the equation, but who is to say? There is surely someone out there who can remote view just like that.

It was an interesting evening and the first time I met Ced Jackson, who joined our London Group. He subsequently gave the talk on *Sacred Geometry* referred to earlier.

CHAPTER SEVENTEEN

Chalking it up to experience

Two of our London members, Clive and Mandy, had been exploring a field near their home in Essex, and thought they might have found a Roman road. Could others in the group go over and dowse the same ground to see whether there was agreement? Moves had been made to get a JCB on site and by the time we arrived, the first few bucketfuls of soil had been looked at. In the spoil was a tegular, part of a Roman tile.

This little dig was watched by several interested local parties and suddenly, dowsing seemed an acceptable idea. With a few more of us on site, it was decided that this was not a Roman road but more likely to be hardstanding from a building of that period. There seemed to be another building of simple layout in the vicinity.

This field is big. Dowsers were all over it like a rash and there seemed to be objects everywhere. With local interest being what it was, a heritage group was set up with a view to a proper excavation with advice from the County Council Archaeology Department. Currently this is a work in progress and we have to be patient.

Kent, as you probably know, is not short of chalk, with the North Downs stretching across the county and chalk quarries everywhere. On my travels, I have been picking up all sorts of information about chalk. We all know that it is the shells of decomposed sea creatures formed over millions of years, but through the ages it has been used by man for a variety of purposes. I have been informed that it was used by farmers in the Middle Ages to spread on the floor of grain stores due to the fact that it has in it the capacity to restrict the growth of mould. Likewise, it was spread on the land to break up clay soils. It was used to keep food cool with a block of chalk cut out to form a small larder. With a door fitted to the front and a recessed top to hold water, as the water evaporated it removed heat from inside, thus creating a cool store.

In medieval times, chalk was often laid down to create a level surface and I have seen this still done today in a new warehouse complex currently being built. Over 500 years ago, not only was the chalk laid down, but if it was thick enough, sour milk would be poured over it and rolled into the floor, creating a hard, almost marble-like finish.

Going from chalk to what often accompanies it, flint, this rock-like substance starts life as a sea sponge. Hard to believe but true.

Kent chalkland is full of manmade holes and some of them are big. In many places the thin topsoil is clay. Farmers do not like clay because it affords little drainage and is either soaking wet or, in hot weather, rock hard. However, under the clay is crumbly absorbent chalk that would break up the clay and make it more friable. The other advantage is that clay is acidic and chalk is alkaline, so by mixing the two together, the ph content of the soil moves closer to neutral, which is better for crop growth.

As you know, if you dig a hole in the garden, the sides fall in, making the hole wider but shallower. So what these farmers did was bore a vertical shaft about 25 feet down, and then dig out the chalk, usually forming three tunnels, each some 15 to 20 feet long, 10 feet high and about 10 feet wide. The chalk went on the land to break up the clay, and any flint found was sold on for building and walling.

This left the problem of filling in the hole and the often-used method was to take a storm-blown tree, cut off the branches and put it crown-first down the hole. The tangle of tree roots helped to block off the top, and with clay fed into what remained of the hole, the ground was levelled and treated as part of the field.

Over the years, people left the land and forgot where the holes were. As time went by, the tree started to rot, houses were built over the old fields, and suddenly big holes started to appear as the rotting process continued.

A farmer I knew asked me to take a look at the grounds of a private house, because a hole had appeared in the lawn. Could I visit in case it was a chalk mine, a dene hole (similar but smaller) or just a natural feature.

On arrival I noticed an upturned wheelbarrow covering a hole in the middle of the lawn. This was the spot I headed for and, dowsing rods at the ready, started to walk round it but about 10 feet from the wheelbarrow.

As I walked, the rods closed at a certain spot, indicating a void. Two or three more steps and they opened up again so, marking it with sticks, there seemed to be a void some 8 feet wide.

Two more of these voids were revealed during my circuit of the barrow, displaying the often-used trefoil pattern for the chambers. Each tunnel was about 25 feet long with a 12-foot gap, floor to roof. Lifting up the wheelbarrow, I could see a nest of rotted wood. This was the upturned tree root, now a couple of feet lower than the lawn.

Armed with this visual information, the property owner decided to fill in the top with some cross timbers and cover it with earth. I would have liked him to open it up, but there was no interest in doing that. One day it will open up all the way down but by then, the current owner will be long gone.

These chalk mines litter the North Downs and are not easy to find. With building space at a premium, I fear there are a few surprises in store for new and future home-owners.

Garden hunt by dowser goes well

WHEN Bill Jordan spotted a wet patch in his garden he assumed it was the start of rising damp.

In desperation he bought a pair of dowsing rods from a novelty shop and decided to try to discover the source.

But his scepticism soon disappeared when the rods started to move and pointed him clearly to where the water was coming from.

Mr Jordan contacted a professional dowser who identified a 15th century well which he and his wife are now having rebuilt.

The pensioner, of Norman Road, Whitstable, said: "Everyone had a laugh over me using the rods but I think I have had the last laugh.

"I have had the water tested by the council and they say I can use it for the garden or washing the car ,which means we can beat the hosepipe ban and help with the water situation.

"I was amazed at what we were able to find out and will be taking these things far more seriously in future."

Mr Jordan was originally inspired to try dowsing after reading about it in a newspaper.

When his efforts proved fruitful he got in touch with the British Society of Dowsers, who provided him with a list of people who could help.

He is now keen for others to try their services.

"There are so many of these old wells about that I really think it is worth people finding out," he said. "Given the droughts we keep getting, anything that can provide another source of water has to be a good thing."

For more information on dowsing visit www.britishdowsers.org

23rd. June 2006
Tel.

Dear John,

As promised, at last, I have the film processed, and enclosing a couple of photos of our WELL. You & Sandy investigated and successfully identified for us here at Duncan Down. The water has been tested by the Council Environmental Services Officer. She confirmed it was safe to use for watering the garden & car washing etc. But not for drinking.

Many thanks once again.

Yours Sincerely,
Kind Regards
Bill Jordan
Kath & Bill JORDAN

CHAPTER EIGHTEEN

Doing Well

It is a similar scenario with wells. Prior to the First World War, most dwellings outside of big cities used a well for drinking water. When a mains water supply was connected to the house, the well was redundant, so what do you do? Fill it gradually with rubbish as some did, or do what most people did which was to salvage the top few feet of brick or stone lining for re-use, as it was a useful commodity, then set timbers on the top of the remaining perimeter wall. The top few feet would be filled in with rubbish (probably artefacts now) and top soil added.

With the advent of droughts becoming more frequent, especially in southern England, more and more people are starting to wonder if their property had an old well and if it could be brought back into use. Often it can, and as long as the well water is taken to the public health laboratories for analysis – usually three samples are needed over a year – and the water is passed clear for drinking, you can save money. If it is not suitable for drinking, it can be used to water the garden or wash the car.

At the time of writing, there have been serious floods across England with water filtration plants put out of action. There must have been quite a few properties not inundated by floods, that had their own wells but which have been covered over, filled in or lost. If these had been accessible, those households would have had water for washing, flushing the toilets and if checked for quality, boiled for drinking. You never know when some disaster or other is

Essex

Telephone :

16th September, 2003

Dear Sirs,

Dowsing for a well at ___________

We are writing on behalf of John Baker, to confirm to you that he dowsed our property for a well and subsequently, when we dug down, the well was found eight feet under the surface.

Yours faithfully,

Christine Papworth

Chris Papworth

Chris and Christine Papworth

For the attention of the British Association of Dowsers

A letter from the proud owner of one of the wells shown in the colour plate section.

likely to strike and to be self-sufficient in water is a gift of some magnitude. Water is the most important commodity we can lay our hands on and to be without it causes the most incredible disruption to our lives.

While on this subject I went to visit a full time water diviner on his home turf to see what I could learn and to confirm or otherwise that I was doing things right. It was pleasing to note that my abilities seemed to be in line with his. Working with another dowser is quite unusual, we are solitary animals when at work and it was great to know I was not missing anything, which is all good for the confidence.

Digging out an old well which could vary in depth from 35 to 70 feet is not to be undertaken lightly, and advice should be sought before embarking on such a project. Very often, I can be invited to a garden and dowse for a well, mark it out, give some idea of its depth, and then be told that it's nice to know we have one and we'll think about what to do next. At which point the idea wanes a bit.

Personally, I'd be fascinated to open up a well as you don't know what you might find. It could be anything from animal (or human!) bones, precious items put down for safe-keeping and never recovered, and all manner of household articles abandoned over the years. As you will see later on, some surprising things come up.

Whilst on the subject of wells, the well itself is only the container. At the bottom is usually a small diameter bore-hole which goes down to the water source proper. When this is cleared, water pressure pushes the H_2O up the pipe into the well and subject to that pressure, the well will fill to its natural level. This will only alter if the water pressure drops, as does happen where there is a variable sub-strata supply.

This once happened with the British Army in India where one camp was so short of water that bowsers had a regular delivery run for the troops. An army Captain found someone who could dowse and when a likely spot for water was found, a well was dug and with the use of pumps, a copious supply of drinking water was enjoyed by all.

It took some weeks for information to filter through that in the local village, supplies of water had mysteriously dried up. It was soon realised that the dowser had tapped into the same supply and the army, with all its mechanical resources, was siphoning it off. To avoid a confrontation with the local farmers, the pumps were turned off and it was back to the bowser delivery.

Chapter Nineteen

Light dawns

On one of my trips to visit the Barnes family, I had been asked to look for an item of costume jewellery which one of their other guests had lost some time previously. It could be anywhere, which included several acres of orchards.

I had begun to realise that I was not too good at finding small objects. I know one or two people who are brilliant at it, to the point where if you send them a plan of a house where something is lost, they will dowse and very often find it. If you don't practise, you never get any better, so I will always have a try.

I was in the orchard with several people including the Barnes' son and daughter-in-law when I started to dowse by direction finding, that is, standing with just one rod and turning in a circle. If I pick up what I'm looking for, the rod will point in the direction of the find even though I am turning, so that gives me the direction in which I should walk.

I had tried this before and reached a point where the item should have been, but a little digging was unsuccessful. I did find a piece of pottery and in fenland soil there is usually nothing, not even a stone.

So this was attempt number two and as I started to dowse, Phil, the daughter-in-law, shot off at a rate of knots back to the house. The speed of this exit obviously registered with me; I know some people get disconcerted by what I do. Despite my best efforts, I drew another blank, although this time a piece of coal came out of the soil, something else which should not have been there.

Some time later, when Phil was on her own in the house, I asked her why she had gone off in such a hurry. "When you started to dowse," she said, "you were surrounded by people." I told her I was already aware of that, but then she said, "Not just those people but *other people* as well. In fact," she continued, "you've got someone with you now. You've always got someone with you."

At that moment I realised that the vision I'd been seeing out of the corner of my eye when I started dowsing years ago was 'someone' keeping a watching brief on me. It all fell into place in a way I cannot describe. And neither can I describe the feeling almost of elation at the thought that I was being looked after. Somehow all the pieces had been lodged in the back of my mind, but now they had fallen into place and I had the full picture. Amazing!

* * * * *

One of my neighbours and his wife were off to Hampshire for a few days and they had always been interested in what I got up to. So on this occasion they asked me if I could find them by map dowsing while they were away. Always keen to get some practice I explained that the only way I could stand a chance of finding them was if they were not moving about, so they said that on one day in particular they would definitely be having lunch between one and two o'clock, so they would be fixed for that hour.

They left a map for me, turned to the section which included Hampshire, so on the allotted day, I sat down and tried to find them by dowsing the map. I then stuck a pin through the page and left it for them to find on their return.

When they got home I was told I was miles out, which was a pity but they seemed more upset about it than me. After all, no one can be a hundred per cent accurate all the time. So that was that until a couple of days later when they called me in to see them and there was the map with my pinhole showing. Apparently, the page was left open with Hampshire on it to help me, but the county continued on to the next page, which was on the reverse side. The pinhole had continued through to the other side of the page and, overleaf, was within a mile of where they had been eating! That was a happy surprise and taught me another lesson – only map dowse on a single-sided sheet because it seems that it is possible to pick up on things on the reverse side.

So why can't we dowse for lost people or someone who has been murdered? Well, maybe some people can, but it would not be wise for them to broadcast it as they could become a target for ne'er do wells. We can only map dowse for people from whom we have had permission to do so. It must be realised that we are not in control and there are rules we have to abide by. To ignore them is to risk losing the ability to dowse and I would *never* do that.

It's fun to ask if you can find someone when they go on holiday. They should just give you the name of the country they are visiting. If it is the US you can dowse for them during British daylight hours as they will be in bed due to the time shift. The less you know of the country, the better your chance of success as your conscious mind is not nagging at you saying, "That's a likely place" or "That's a popular holiday resort", and it's quite a thrill when you get it right.

Stapleford
Cambridge

5th June 2006

Dear John,

thank you very much for taking the time to dowse the map of the historic site for me. The position you marked as a well, on closer inspection at the site revealed a man hole cover & water chamber of some description. I haven't designed any planting on the 'black line'!

Kind regards Julia Weaver

More finds through map dowsing, with postcards from an excited resident and (opposite) the plan John used to discover the whereabouts of the well.

Stapleford
Cambridge

24 Sept. 2006

Dear John,

Apologies for the time delay. thanks again for your time and assistance. Enclosed is a copy of the map we used

Kind regards

Julia Weaver

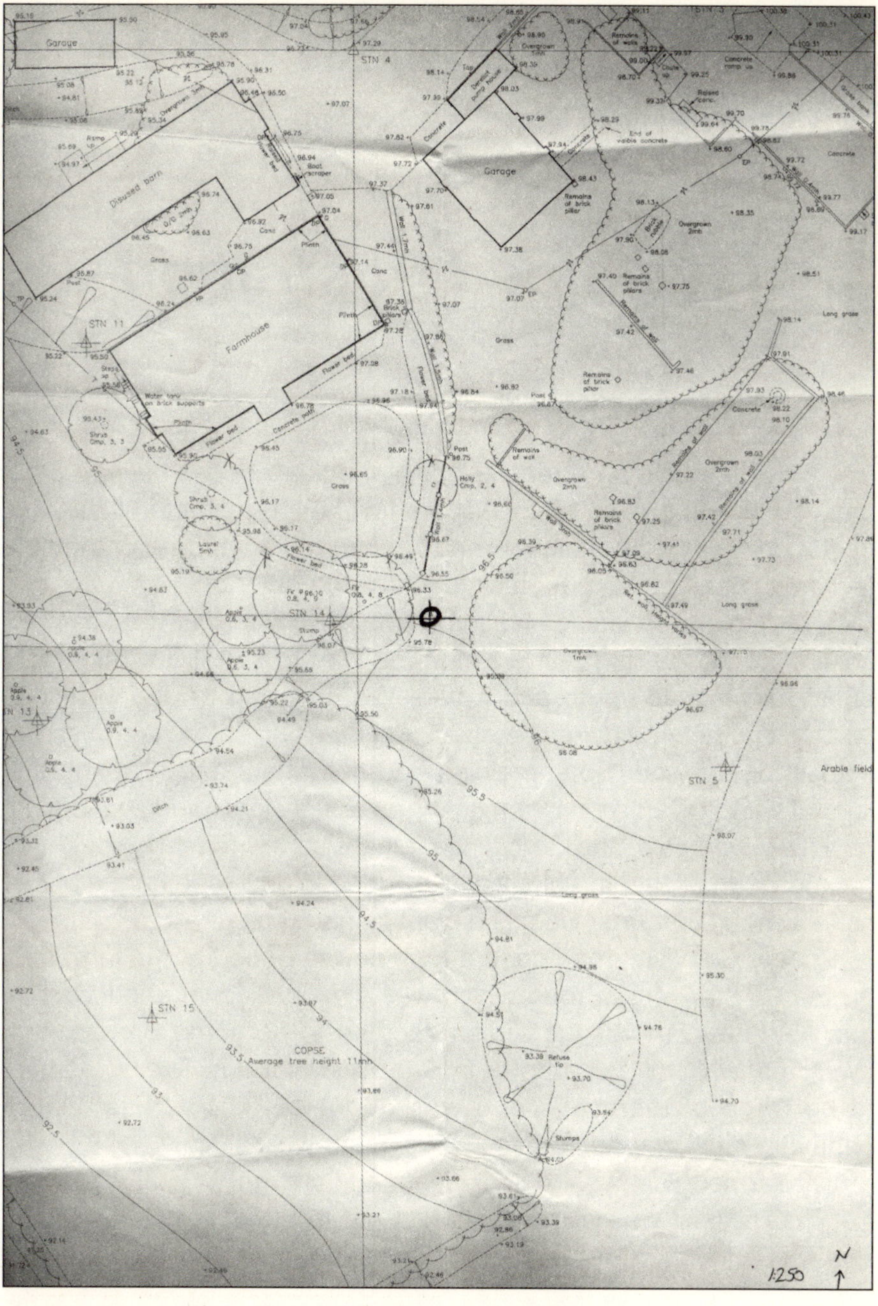

Garage
STN 4
Disused barn
Farmhouse
Flower bed
Concrete path
Grass
STN 11
Garage
Concrete
Remains of brick pillar
Overgrown 2mh
Remains of wall
Long grass
Concrete
Holly
Laurel
Flower bed
STN 14
Stump
Apple
STN 13
Ditch
STN 5
Arable field
Long grass
Refuse tip
Stumps
STN 15
COPSE
Average tree height 11mh
N
1:250

Chapter Twenty

Five-sided frustration

Time to phone our farmer and see if the pentagon has had any effect on his crops. The answer is that he hadn't had time to visit the field on a regular basis and there doesn't seem to be any variation in growth rates. Apparently the thermometer within the pentagon was giving a higher reading than the outer one for the first few days, but then slipped back to match the other one.

This was disappointing and some time later, when we went back to collect the kit we had left, our first job was to see if the pentagon effect had moved south and it had! We now had to go inside the pointed end before finding the effect and it was south of the two sticks across the flat end. So something had gone right and although the idea of warming an area by thought processes alone did seem odd, it obviously worked in the Scilly Isles, otherwise the farmers would not have gone to all that trouble. It was decided to have another go in the spring when the farmer would be planting his crops.

Prior to our visit, I had done a map dowse of part of the farm and picked up the Roman road which was already known about, but in one field near a river there also seemed to be some Bronze Age dwellings, which we started to look for and plot out. There seemed to be three of them and one was about 40 feet across with a perimeter ditch and an opening on its south-west side.

The farmer was keen to investigate and brought in a JCB to dig a trench. The soil was alluvial, not clay as in the surrounding fields, and we had high hopes of finding something, but after going down a couple of feet we seemed to be hitting natural earth. We should have cut across a ditch and found part of the hut floor, but there was nothing. This field was close to the junction of two rivers and the thought was that over the centuries, whatever had been there was over time washed away. This was disappointing as everything made sense. We had a phone call a few months later to say that a Bronze Age burial site had been found in the next field, but no sign of the dwelling area.

Members of my local archaeological group were hoping to move onto a farm where a medieval priory building was known to have existed. I dowsed the area and could not find anything structural under the ground. The area we would have preferred to dig was a cow field and the cows bunched up at one end behind some sheds for protection from the elements. The ground was thick mud with giant stinging nettles enjoying the fresh fertiliser they were constantly getting. I had tried to get into the area but it was no use, so I asked for a plan of the farm and sat down to map dowse.

I noted there were walls going in all directions and that they were fourteenth-, fifteenth-, sixteenth- and eighteenth-century. This was as far as I could go and it was put aside for the time being. The (to me) unpromising site was started on and what a lot of rubbish was found. If you ever dowse farmland, watch out for rubbish buried by farmers over the years. We found corrugated iron, a lot of sinks, rubber tyres and, at about five feet down, some eighteenth-century crockery stacked in a neat line. We also found some stone blacking jars, one of which came from the site where Charles Dickens worked as a boy in a factory adjacent to what is now London's Charing Cross station.

By this time I had been water divining with enough results to be put on the BSD register, so I now had two strings to my bow. While I would never earn any money on the archaeology side, I could now charge people who wanted me to find water for them.

Some of the places I have been to and the successes I have had are not included in this book because they are quite ordinary. When things go smoothly it isn't much of a story! What surprises me is that the people I visit are so trusting and I can see how charlatans get away with things. I always tell the people for whom I dowse that they should bear in mind I have dowsed a spot where I believe something to be, but until proven it is just the twitching of two rods. No system is foolproof and I can have an off day just like anyone else. People ask how successful I am and the answer is that if you bet against me, you would lose money.

Chapter Twenty-one

BSD Debut

Up to now, the archaeological side of dowsing has been somewhat limited in appeal and had no great following in the BSD although a few members had been working at it for years. So I was quite surprised to be asked one day if, at the next Congress, would I mind talking to some other members about what I had been doing. That was fine with me, I've never had a problem talking; whether it made any sense or not was a different matter.

I envisaged a few people sitting having a fireside chat before the main events took place. Then, a week before the Congress was due to open, I received a telephone call asking if I needed any help with getting information sheets printed? Did I need the overhead projector? Was I using slides? I couldn't understand why all this was needed for a few people but then came the bombshell.

The interest had been so great that the main lecture hall was to be used and so far, seventy people had intimated that they wanted to sit in on the talk. There would be six speakers and I was going to be on last with a twenty minute spot. I had to sit down and think about this, my vision of a nice little chat was well and truly out of the window. Speaking in front of an audience has never bothered me before but being the last speaker, what was I going to be left with to talk about? Everyone else would have got in first.

Over the years I had brought together a series of slides and now I had to pull them into some sort of shape. I had never used a slide projector and this was more of a concern. By the time the Congress came round I was past worrying and in the lecture theatre I found myself with people who had many more years experience than me. There was the usual panic, one of the projectors – mine – decided to play up but as I was last on, I was in a position to gain some insight into how or how not to give a talk of this nature.

As each speaker went through their talk it was apparent that if you need notes, the flow of what you are saying is broken and people's attention starts to wander. Luckily, I've always got away without using them, I just open my mouth and hope for the best. More good news was the fact that the previous speaker operated the projector for the next person and being last, I did not have to worry about that.

My turn came and off I went but I had not completed my talk when the twenty minutes was up. I took another ten minutes to finish. Although we were all speaking on the same subject, we each approached things in a different manner and my fear of repetition was unfounded.

The evening was rounded off with a questions and answers session which was enjoyable and the whole thing went off really well. The mastermind behind this was one Sue Brown who was to have a big part to play in future events, and whom I was fated to work with in the future, as will be seen.

A few days after the Congress, I was asked whether I would like to promote an Archaeological Special Interest Group (SIG) for the UK and Eire, and become its first chairman. This came as a surprise and as I worked for a living, albeit my own company which could give me room for manoeuvre, it was a question of whether I could do it justice. Persuaded by Sue Brown, I said I would give it a go and if I wasn't able to get things moving, someone else could take over.

At about the same time I had a telephone call from the head of the Portuguese Dowsing Group, Radethesia Lusitania. Would I be interested in going to Portugal to teach archaeological dowsing to some of their members? Thinking the chances of this happening would be slight, I said yes, providing I had plenty of notice.

Chapter Twenty-two

Jane Goldman investigates

Being the London Group for dowsing, we get a number of enquiries from the media, either direct or passed on to us from the Malvern office. The media have a bad habit of having their own agenda, and great care is needed to discover the real motive for their interest. It is so easy to be sent up and made to look foolish as some journalists regard dowsing as a bit of a lark that no one in their right mind would take seriously.

Now and again a company would satisfy us that they were *bona fide* and Flame Productions was one of the genuine ones. They were doing a television series called *Jane Goldman Investigates*, where each week she investigated some aspect of the paranormal. Not that dowsing is paranormal to dowsers.

Jane was going to spend a month researching each subject. She had already arranged to be taught the basics of dowsing but she needed to actually find something that could be proved. The immediate thought was the well in Essex which we were sure was there but had not yet been investigated. The owner was also keen to find proof. With film company money on offer, this was the time to do it, so we arranged for Jane to visit the site and I would keep an eye on things in case help was needed, and also do some map dowsing with her.

Some time later one of my neighbours called to say that Jane would be on a television chat show, which I think was Richard and Judy. Appearing with her was a clairvoyant who told her to watch out for a barn on fire, at which she looked somewhat bemused. It was interesting to see who I was going to meet in a few weeks time.

In the meantime the London Group was going from strength to strength with membership rising to over thirty with a good mix of people, four of them had doctorates and it was interesting to see how they used dowsing in their own specialised ways.

Our web site was constantly attracting new members but London has a transient population so people come and go all the time, hopefully spreading the word wherever they move to, which in many cases is abroad.

In most groups there is usually someone you find difficult to get on with but so far I was enjoying the company of all the members, they were a really nice bunch of people and the meetings were a joy to be part of, always with something unusual happening.

One day a neighbour asked if I could find out the date of the plaster head of a lion which he had found deep in the bowels of a bomb site in London. It looked pretty smoke-blackened and my first thought was London grime had got to it over the years, but it was plaster and had horse hair sticking out of the back.

I tried to dowse a date, working backwards from the present but at 1700 I stopped because I was getting no reaction. This is where I learnt to always work up from the furthest distance, so with no idea of its place in history, I went back to the Roman period. Working up through the centuries to 1600, the rod started to move and it reached the find position at 1666. This was the date of the Great Fire of London. That was why it was so smoke-blackened. I was later told the site was near London's Cannon Street station, which was Great Fire territory.

At our very next meeting, I decided to ask one of the members, Mick Spicer, if he could find a date for it. He is very good at psychometry, something barely mentioned yet. He lifted the head from its box and straight away said, "This was in the Great Fire of London." Collapse of other parties, as they used to say in earlier times. More on psychometry later.

A few weeks later I was invited to give a talk to a historical group that had at the rear of their meeting hall a piece of ground where a building had once stood, so it would be ideal for members to have a try at dowsing afterwards.

On the day of the meeting several rows of those horrible plastic chairs which are very slippery and slidy were in place, and I was to stand behind a table to do my talk.

As people filtered in, it was becoming apparent that more chairs would be needed. As they added chairs to the front rows, so the distance between me and my audience was diminishing fast. And still they came, so the table was set against the wall and I was to stand in front of it.

I started with my usual background to the subject and as everyone was keen to get some practise in afterwards I moved on to the relaxation part described previously. This soon brought us to where people started to hold out their arms. The person who had invited me, Jeff, was perched on a chair in the far corner of the room.

Everyone except Jeff now had their eyes closed and as I got to the bit where I expected arms to reach out, nothing happened, which surprised me somewhat. The lady sitting immediately in front of me was wearing a long tartan skirt, and she gradually began to slide off her seat until her legs slipped either side of mine. She was spark out! And I could not move!! I looked at Jeff and he calmly intimated that I should carry on.

I thought the lady was dead. Her involuntary slide off the seat had been felt by the people sitting either side of her, and they struggled to pull her up. I am still going on with my talk. Gradually others in the room began to realise that something was going on, and then the ambulance came. Dah-dah dah-dah! Well by this time I had lost my audience entirely and they all watched fascinated as this woman was carried from the room.

I had visions of newspaper headlines, DOWSER KILLS ELDERLY LADY, and big stories such as IS DOWSING DANGEROUS?

After the hubbub died down, Jeff said to me, “Don’t worry, it’s happened before.” I thought well thanks very much, I wish I’d known beforehand. I think the rest of the evening passed off alright, but even to this day, what happened afterwards remains a bit of a blur.

A Kent chalk mine, many of which have been 'lost' with the entrance shaft obliterated, but which can suddenly reappear as the 'plug' rots away. Most chalk mines are smaller than this one but some form large galleries.
Photo: Nick Catford

Rediscovering an old well. The top few feet of this well surround had been removed when it was sealed up many years earlier.

Dowsing has highlighted the possible site of an earlier building. The flag markers and red-and-white tape show the outline.

Not a promising start to the dowsed well.

No sign of a top surround, just solid clay.

Two days later, the hole had filled with water.

Despite a lengthy period of dry, hot weather, the water level was maintained.

After further digging, plus the fitting of concrete 'O' rings down the shaft, this well is brought back into use. The property was built without knowledge of the well and almost ended up covering it.

This is the well featured in the Jane Goldman Investigates – Dowsing *TV programme. It shows how much of a feature can be made of these old wells.*

The cross we found down the well, unfortunately broken in one place. Although we are not quite sure, we feel it must have been the village cross, perhaps stolen and disposed of down the well.

This was a dowsing project where the search was on for the end wall of a building. When excavated, the wall had been almost completely 'robbed' out. In some circumstances, dowsing can discover a wall that has been completely robbed, but evidence that it was there is shown by later infill.

Satellite photographs of the meteorite site in Bolivia.

Top right: *The general area around the Rio Madidi and showing the Ojaki Crater. The nearest civilisation was probably La Paz.*

Centre left: *The meteorite crater.*

Bottom right: *The lip of the crater.*

Used with the kind permission of the Scientific Exploration Society (SES)
For more information visit
www.ses-explore.org/Page1.aspx?PageID=2022

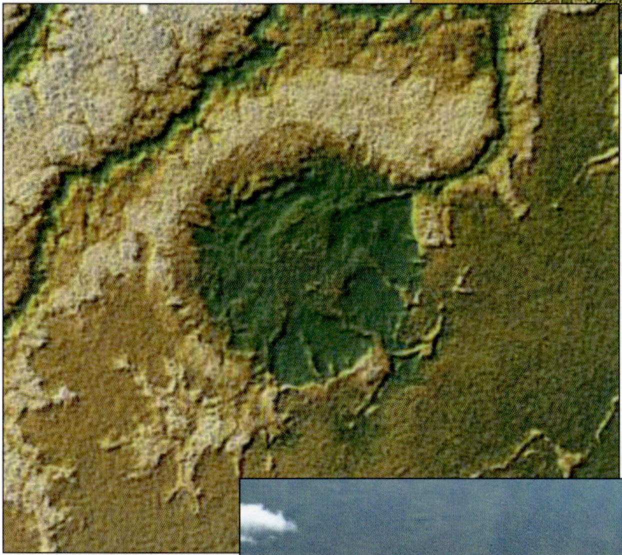

Our dowser is looking for a copper pipe. She is standing with the rods in the find position.

As she gets nearer to the pipe, the rods start to cross . . .

. . . and are at right angles to her body when she is over what she is looking for.

As she walks on, the rods begin to uncross and will eventually open up as in the first picture.

CHAPTER TWENTY-THREE

Going up in the world

It's a strange thing but when people earn a lot of money they like to go up in the world, both metaphorically and in real terms. When they've moved to the top of a hillside or command a distant view, the next thing they want is a swimming pool, probably followed by a pond or in some cases a lake. Of course, being at the top of a hill they are furthest away from a water supply, and this is where the water diviner comes in.

The client will have already made numerous enquiries about water supplies from the local water board and neighbouring farmers. They have almost certainly drawn a blank, so you appear with a forked stick or a pair of dowsing rods and the owner of several acres of land explains the need for a pond, or a swimming pool or even a lake, and wants to know if you can find a reliable supply of water?

Over ninety per cent of the world's drinkable water is underground but that does not mean you can dig a hole just anywhere. So here I am with my client who would like access to water there, there and there, as it would be close to a power supply for the pump. I start my search and I am finding water at 200 feet here and at another spot it is showing at a similar depth. At this point I am told that the local water board has a borehole two miles away at 220 feet, so my client now has more confidence in me but he is not happy. Could it be possible to find water closer to the surface? I try a third spot but this time it is at 240 feet, so there would appear to be water at the three places I have dowsed and duly marked with spray paint.

That is the end of the exercise; it is now down to the client to decide whether to risk anything up to £16,000 on having a borehole drilled. This may seem a lot of money but for a big pond with no run off supply and high summer evaporation, this sum would soon be recovered.

A few weeks later, I received a phone call from my client, the news is bad. He has had the driller in and no water has been found but, and here was the good news, the bore was not put down at any of the three places I had checked out. This I could not understand, why call me in, pay me good money and then ignore the advice given? As the saying goes, "There's nowt so queer as folk". I was invited back to see if the borehole had been drilled a bit deeper, would it have found water?

I now get the full story. It was assumed that, since I had dowsed for and found water in the three proposed and marked spots, that there would be water everywhere in between too. Not so. I am now asked to check the borehole to see if water is so close that it would just mean taking the bore a little further so that the expense could be justified. At 270 feet I am still going through solid ground, not a twitch from rods or forked stick. No point in going further. Another couple of spots are checked and once again show nothing. The next finds water at 190 feet and at that point the exercise ends. It is really frustrating when you give time and effort to help someone, only for them to ignore the results. Luckily, most people go with what you come up with and are all the happier with the outcome.

This next little story relates to a certain lady in my life who, for my own wellbeing, I will refer to as Amy, because she was so amiable about what happened. I was telling her one winter's day about an experiment that had been done on non-retinal vision and how with your hands only you could, for example, tell the colour of something without any visual clues. She was somewhat sceptical about this so I offered to prove to her that it was possible. This next bit is X rated.

I slipped my hands up under her jumper and cupped her bra. I was met with a look of pleasant bemusement at this and with a happy smile on my face after a few seconds I told her that the bra she was wearing was blue.

As Amy could not remember which one she had put on that morning, a look at the strap showed it was indeed blue. This was regarded as luck which suited me because over the next few winter weeks when clothing was rather more substantial, I proceeded to demonstrate that it was not luck. If my memory serves me correctly, there were about five of these episodes when I got the colour right each time.

Of course, if the lady in your life is devoted to Marks & Spencer's white, there is not much point in trying it, but Amy was into different colours, with the exception of green. I thought afterwards, if I had known about this when I was in my late teens, I could have had a whale of a time, and probably been arrested! I would add, ladies, that I am available to demonstrate this knack at any time. Please form an orderly queue. Say what you like, dowsing is never boring!

On a more respectable note, as I was now Chairman of the Special Interest Group (SIG) for Archaeology, the BSD Council felt I should become a member of Council as well. Since things were going well with Sue Brown pulling the strings, it was to be put forward at the next Congress for a vote. I should explain that the British Society of Dowsers is a registered charity and therefore Council is responsible for the way the charity is run in accordance with certain rules and regulations.

Things were really on the move now and for me, doors just kept on opening. My knowledge of the other members was quite limited but they seemed to have a lot of letters after their names, so I hoped I would not be out of my depth.

In the late spring it was time to go back to Richard, the farmer trying the pentagon effect again and this time we were better prepared. We had access to earth thermometers called data loggers from an agricultural college. These were to be placed in the soil for a month, one inside the pentagon and one outside. Information would then be downloaded onto a computer and the readout presented to us.

Richard had arranged for some borage seed to be sown in this field because it was fast growing and would quickly show any variation between inside and outside the pentagon. On the day, we assembled and put in the big wooden stakes with the pointed end of the pentagon facing north. This created a space measuring about 25 feet by 15 feet. We walked through the pentagon with dowsing rods in the find position but did not pick up any movement at all. This done, we walked round the edge of the markers with the intent that the area inside would become warmer than outside. As each circuit was completed, we noticed that the rod started to turn inward. After five circuits, the rod had swung across my body, indicating that I had completed what I had to do.

My two companions in this, Vicky and Clive, carried out the same operation and with a request for the farmer to again top up the intent by walking around it once a week, we left.

That spring there was a drought, the borage shrivelled up and as before, our farmer did not have the time to carry out the topping up exercise. However, we still had the data loggers in place and after about a month, Clive returned to the farm to remove them and get them analysed. The news was not good. Although the data logger inside the pentagon showed a slightly higher reading than the outer one, it was not statistically significant. Oh dear! More disappointment.

I still feel this experiment is worth carrying on with as our farmers in the Scilly Isles would not have gone to all that trouble if it had not worked for them. In our experiments, we did find that the effect moved south, which is what happened to them. Also, when we created the effect initially and walked through the pentagon with dowsing rods in the find position, the moment we entered the area, the rods crossed and they didn't uncross until after we left the other side. So something has happened. It bugs me and, like a dog with a bone, I am not going to leave it alone.

Chapter Twenty-Four

Loved Avebury, pity about Stonehenge

The London Group has been growing, with our pub venue proving a great success although it has been a bit noisy at times with people in other parts of the pub being rather loud, but overall it has been a good move with membership up to fifty plus. Luckily they don't all turn up for the same meeting, as our room holds about thirty-five in comfort.

With six meetings a year it has often been difficult to get speakers as our subject is quite exclusive in many ways. We have had talks on auras, remote viewing, water divining in Africa, and relaxation and self hypnosis, with some of our own more talented members taking the floor from time to time.

One week we had a trip to Avebury and Stonehenge which took some organising as Stonehenge is by appointment only if you want access to the stone circle itself. We were given a time-slot of 7 pm for three-quarters of an hour which in July was fine. The day was a scorcher with wall to wall sunshine and on reaching Avebury, we all decanted and went our various ways.

Never having been to either site before, I was interested in seeing if I would get any reaction to my dowsing rods from the stones. The place was busy and, starting on the inside of one of the big circles, I found as I approached a stone, the single rod I was holding turned in towards the centre. This happened every time I passed a stone, but if I went behind the stones, on the outside of the circle, there was no reaction. I found this interesting, as did other people, and it was not long before other visitors were getting rods out of their backpacks and joining in. They had been waiting for someone to start and suddenly there were rods everywhere!

One of our members borrowed a rod from me and found the same thing happened, but by the time he had tried it on two or three stones, he handed the rod back to me saying that it was taking all the energy out of him. This from someone who was a swimming instructor who had swum the English Channel.

As you may know, Avebury has two big circles and I believe one or possibly two small ones inside them. Moving on to the second large circle I was amazed to find that this time the rod swung out from the centre but again, no reaction if I walked round the back of the stones.

I was getting a positive and a negative circle and if memory serves me correctly, the two smaller circles did the same, so which came first? Did the stones create the positive and negative effect or was the effect there to start with and ancient man tuned in to this and placed the stones as markers? If you get the chance to visit Avebury, try it for yourself, the effect is quite strong.

Other members of our group found that certain stones seemed to cause different reactions. One person wanted to curl up and go to sleep when he reached one particular stone. I know we are dealing with people who are sensitive to certain situations but you too may be susceptible to some of these energies. Give it a try.

After a long and interesting afternoon at Avebury, it was back to the coach and on to Stonehenge. At seven in the evening there are very few people around and with the sun melting into a golden sunset, the place was bathed in a really atmospheric light, so what would we experience here?

I have seen Stonehenge on TV many times and the scale of it always seems impressive. Yet walking among the stones, the whole place seems to have shrunk and I can't think of any other situation where television makes something look bigger than it actually is. Seeing the place first hand, I have to say I did not get any buzz out of it at all, despite the atmospheric conditions. My rods weren't getting any reaction to the stones or their layout with just one small exception, a large stone with quartz in it.

One or two others in our party picked up on bits and pieces but nobody seemed to be in awe of the place. I think that on the day, Avebury was the favourite site.

I don't get too involved in earth energies as some dowsers do, it is a bit too esoteric for me, but I do pick up these things and often come across ley lines, energy and black lines. Perhaps I should explain. Ley lines are supposed to be lines of energy which go straight across country and often link up ancient sites. Now a good dowser can create a ley line and I'm surprised organisations like the SAS don't use it.

Of course, any line that is created must be removed. We have to be responsible about this. Energy lines run in pairs or pairs of pairs, so they are easy to identify. Black lines are energy again but usually bad news if your house is built over one, although they can be removed.

* * * * *

My Sunday mornings at this time were taken up with a dig by my local archaeology group and an interesting bunch they are. Apart from doing some dowsing on site from time to time, and maybe trying to date an artefact that has been unearthed, I am just one of the infantry with shovel, fork and trowel.

People from all walks of life who have an interest in local history are represented and some of them are very knowledgeable. Amateur they may be, but in the way Patrick Moore was an amateur astronomer. Midway through the morning there would be a stop for tea and usually, Jaffa Cakes.

It is here that I have to thank the Director of the group, Chris Baker, for letting me get involved in the first place, as many archaeologists regard dowsers as Dracula regards daylight. I have no idea why, it seems daft to me, as any input a dowser can give should be added to other available information. It helps to get a better idea of what may be under ground. A landscape painter would not go out without cobalt blue in his palette; he needs all the colours to get a proper picture. Luckily, there is some shift in attitude but it is hard work.

CHAPTER TWENTY-FIVE

Flame Productions and the barn in flames

At last I have a date for when Flame Productions want to get Jane Goldman to hopefully find the well as the climax to her programme, *Jane Goldman Investigates – Dowsing.*

The meeting is arranged for one o'clock on a Saturday afternoon and I arrange to be on the site of the alleged well somewhat earlier, in order to do a plan of the shingle yard. Jane can then have a go at map dowsing the area before the site work begins.

On arrival, the area looks completely different to when I last saw it, so much so that I had to dowse the position of the well again and make a mental note of where it was. I then drew a plan of the yard with some measurements added so that she would have an idea of the scale of things.

That done I went to the pub where we were to meet, but received a message saying the film crew were running late. As I sat outside the pub with a drink, a massive pall of smoke appeared over the rooftops of the houses opposite, quickly followed by the sound of fire engine sirens. One, two, three of them raced by, it looked like a big fire, but after half an hour or so, the smoke disappeared. I went inside to get another drink and asked the barman, "What was that all about?"

"It was the farm a short distance away. Apparently their barn had caught fire."

I immediately thought back to the TV programme where the psychic had warned Jane Goldman about a barn catching fire. If she and the film crew had been on time, they would have witnessed it!

Eventually the crew arrived with Vicky Sweetlove from the London Dowsers who had spent the morning with Jane, showing her how to map dowse for water, and it was at this point Vicky handed over to me.

It was a hot day, so we sat down to lunch first and then Jane started to map dowse the position of the well on the plan I had drawn. She seemed to be quite close, which was impressive as it is easy to get it wrong, then off we went to the shingle yard just next door to the pub.

The dowsing rods she had were a bit lightweight and the wind was blowing them about, so I handed her mine. They are heavy but there is no ambiguity about them, when they move you know there is something there. This was crunch time, because all we had to go on was the movement of two rods, there had been no other investigation. On top of that, the film crew had brought a small piece of drilling equipment so they really meant business.

Jane started off with a little bit of direction finding, then started walking and came quite close to the spot I had dowsed earlier. My thoughts of maybe having to find it for her were beginning to fade; she really seemed to have acquired the knack over the last four weeks with other dowsers.

Eventually, she found a point where the rods crossed, and was quite emphatic about this being where the well would be found. Cue the drilling equipment.

After several attempts the drilling rig refused to work so, in order to try to retrieve something from the situation, the owner of the site set about with a shovel, moving a few inches of gravel and then probing the spot with a ten-foot scaffold pole. With a bit of effort, the pole started to go down far more readily than it would have if the ground had been solid. It looked as if we had all picked the right spot, but it was still not fully proven.

Over the course of the next few weeks, the owner made the hole deeper and there was the definite outline of something circular although the brick or stone which would have surrounded the well was missing. It was then arranged for someone to come in and dig out the hole. Some time later I received a telephone call to say that there *was* a well there and it was about 27 feet deep. The artefacts discovered consisted mainly of old beer pots, as the place had originally been a coaching inn.

One surprise was a stone cross that had unfortunately been broken in two (*see colour plate section*). It was about two feet in diameter and some seven inches thick. The stone was very smooth and not native to this part of the world, which has no quarries for miles. It was extremely heavy but not at all weathered. Trying some psychometry on it gave the impression that it was the proceeds of looting at some time in the distant past. Various experts have since studied it but no conclusion has been reached. The best idea is that it may have been the village cross.

This is the thing about wells, you never know what has been placed, dropped or thrown down them in the past. It could be the family silver, hidden away for protection, or the remains of a murder victim.

If you have a well, don't ignore it. Open it up and see what's down it, but it must be done with great care. Get advice first.

Chapter Twenty-six

Hoping for a date

Psychometry is something I have touched on before and my understanding is that it is a means of getting information from an object simply by holding it. I know of one person who can usually 'turn it on' without too much trouble and my mentor, Dan Wilson, was a whiz at it.

I have tried it a couple of times. On the site of a dig and sticking out of the side of the hole, I once found a ring, quite plain except for a tiny piece of glass in a clasp. When I got it home I decided to try psychometry on it.

After a good meal and in a relaxed state of mind, I sat down with it and, eyes shut, just let my mind go blank. I started to get the picture of a man, which was a shock because my assumption was that it belonged to a lady. This man was tall, slim and wore a long leather coat and boots, all dark brown. He wore a similar coloured wide-brimmed hat. With this in mind, I looked in a history book which showed how people dressed at certain times in the past, and the period for my gentleman seemed to be when the Pilgrim Fathers set sail for America.

When I asked Dan to see what he could get out of it, I was pleased when he said it had belongd to a man, and he described similar garments except his were black, but so what, the man could have had more than one set of clothes. Dan went on to say that the man was an apothecary who was upset at losing his ring because the green glass was at that time something a bit special.

On another occasion I was given a small pair of very old scissors and tried psychometry on them. My mind led me to an elderly lady, a glove-maker who was working in an upper-floor room with a window overlooking a grassed area with trees. I was getting a very good picture, to the point where I realised things were very quiet and I was aware of the smell of lavender. What, I asked myself, was the reason for the lavender? The answer flashed into my mind that there was a lot of leather in the room, and the scent from the lavender masked its smell.

Whether this is some way of getting flashbacks from holding an object or just the mind on autopilot I do not know, but I find it intriguing. Someone else could get a different response from the same scissors, especially if they tuned in to a different period in the scissor's history. It is something I will try again from time to time and maybe you could try it on a family heirloom.

* * * * *

Off to Malvern for my first Council meeting, not knowing what to expect. With some of the other members of Council unknown to me, I decided to just keep my head down and listen. I had a report to give on what was happening with the archaeological SIG for the UK which, thanks to Sue Brown, was really getting going.

Our meeting was in the BSD offices and shop and it was a bit of a squeeze getting about ten people round a small table. There were Minutes from the last meeting and other bits of business including updates from the education sub-committee.

It was only then I began to realise I was involved in a quite significant and professional organisation, with input from people about advertising, cash flow, the cost of producing the Journal, plans for new courses up and down the country, membership applications and also members who wished to go on the professional register who all had to be checked out to ensure they had *bona fide* references.

Fortunately no one had any wish to drone on about their particular subject and the list of items for discussion was dealt with in a regular and speedy manner, which was just as well because this meeting was held on a Sunday morning and getting back into London on a Sunday afternoon and evening means joining a queue twenty miles from where you want to get to.

Overall I enjoyed the company of the other Council members and looked forward to the next meeting which was to be in three months time. That would be after my adventures in Portugal.

CHAPTER TWENTY-SEVEN

Hot Rods in Portugal

I had received another email from Portugal. It was from José Alexander Cotta, asking me when I can go out to Portugal to teach dowsing and for how long? As I have a business to run, getting away is quite difficult, but the invitation is not one to turn down lightly, never having been to Portugal. I am informed that José speaks very good English and can therefore interpret for me. As luck would have it, two of our London members are Portuguese and they offered to translate some of my notes to send on ahead. After some further correspondence it was agreed that I will fly out over a Spring Bank Holiday. I don't know what I am letting myself in for but it should be interesting.

So it was off to Portugal. It's not very often a proposed trip comes to fruition but it was real this time. I had two days of teaching and was then promised a day's sightseeing with José to be my permanent guide. The good thing is that Portugal is on the same time zone as the UK, so there wouldn't be any problems with jetlag.

I arrived at Porto airport late afternoon, an enormous place with not much going on. It was the end of May and quite hot. José drove me north to the little town of Carminha where I was checked in to a hotel for the night. The place was empty, it was a Thursday night and we went into the town for a meal.

My first impressions of Portugal were that it has done very well out of Euro money, yours and mine. Everywhere we drove was on dual carriageways and hardly a vehicle to be seen. A lot of Carminha

John dowsing with students in Portugal with, as always, rods at the ready.
Photo courtesy of Carlos Fonseca

looks brand new with fountains in the town square and fancy lights in the evening. Again, apart from the locals, there was nobody much about. The food was great and so was the company, so it was a good start. What would tomorrow bring?

The first get together was with about a dozen people in a large room over a health-food shop. The mix was of architects, chemists and other professionals plus a wicker man who spoke no English and I no Portuguese, but for some reason we seemed to get on well with each other. I was introduced to his girlfriend who I assumed spoke good English as the first thing she said to me was that he was a bastard! She certainly liked this bastard.

I have never worked with an interpreter before, but it was a bit like the comedy sketch where the English version is short and the translation twice as long. I was lucky insofar as one other person there spoke excellent English and a couple of others knew a few words, so I spent the morning showing the different dowsing instruments and their effects.

We had lunch in the health-food shop kitchen which, not being too keen on health food, was not really to my taste but it filled a hole. As in Spain, meals go on a bit and the temperature was climbing, so it was with some reluctance that we all set off to walk up the hill to a Roman fort that overlooked the town, and where I was going to do my first practical archaeological course with them to try and find walls below the existing ground level.

One of my associates once described working with a group of dowsers as like trying to herd cats and this is so true. In seconds they were off all over the place and it took some effort to get people to concentrate on what I was trying to get them to do. After a couple of hours, the heat was so much that we all retreated down to the town for drinks and some shade.

So far, things were going all right, I was getting lots of questions which is always a good sign. At the end of a tiring afternoon it was back to the still empty hotel for some cold beers and an evening meal.

Day two started in a similar way and I was planning to touch on map dowsing. To this end I had brought the plan of a small town in which I knew something had been discovered in a certain spot but was not shown. However, an archaeologist in the group had other ideas. He was working on the site of a very old monastery and had brought along a large plan which showed what they had unearthed so far. Like most old buildings, some parts were still standing, but others had long gone. So, could I map dowse this plan? My neck was really on the line now. You could feel the tension in the room as I started to work my way across the plan. On my first sweep of the upper part I could find nothing that was not already shown.

Working my way across the lower section, I started to get a reaction. The baby dowsing rod I was using started to swing inwards, so I made a mark at that point. On my next sweep down the page it moved again so I drew a pencil line between the two.

At this juncture there was a great hubbub in the room and, not speaking the lingo, I had to ask José what is the problem? I was told I have started to show the line of a wall which the archaeologists had found earlier but had not had time to draw in. Based on this, my standing rose immediately and from there on, any doubts about me seemed to disappear. I was on a roll.

A few of us went to lunch at a little café/bar that did fish Moroccan-style. The portions were huge and the fish was cut so that sections of orange were inserted along its length. Sitting there feeling bloated, and with the still hot weather, the idea of more site dowsing did not appeal, but off we went to a place further up in the hills. It proved impractical to dowse but I managed to get stung by something which caused my ankle to swell up, so it was off to the pharmacy for medication.

As a result of the map dowsing success, I was asked if I would go to the monastery the next day, my sightseeing day, to see what I could find on site. They also invited me to work with another of their members, Ricardo, and try to get him into site dowsing. With all that planned it was back to the hotel for more cold beer and an evening meal.

The next day José took me to the town of Guimaraes where we met up with Ricardo and two others of the group, Carlos and Sonia, who spoke excellent English. After another heavy long lunch we all set off into the hills and it seemed hotter than ever. Into sight came this enormous monastery in the middle of nowhere. It was utterly quiet. Entering the big wooden gates, there was a large courtyard surrounded by cloisters, and in the middle was a great big hand-dug hole. In the bottom were some really impressive footings. The question was, could I find the line of the unexposed footings to save an awful lot of digging?

Well, Ricardo struggled with the new art of dowsing and I walked about seeming to get some sensible lines which he marked with string. The others in the party had more sense and stayed in the shade. After a couple of hours, the heat took its toll and we headed back to town where we spent a leisurely late afternoon drinking and enjoying another big meal. We left Guimaraes at about 10 o'clock in the evening and the temperature was still 28ºC. On the way back to Carminha we drove through the smoke from a forest fire and it wasn't even summer yet.

Returning to London I felt the trip had been really worthwile. The people had been very friendly and the food seemed to appear by conveyor belt. I had had an excellent host and although tiring, I had enjoyed the whole experience. Somewhere to return to at some point.

Chapter Twenty-eight

Dowsing the dead

With Portugal behind me it was back to the more mundane world of finding water in some form or other, but once again the unexpected popped up in a request from a Borough Council to see if I could find a section of a graveyard which did not have bodies in it, in order that a garden of remembrance could be created.

Apparently, the land had been used over many years and some of the area was now grassed over with no records as to whether burials had taken place there or not. Due to the ground being quite flinty in nature, resistivity machines like you see on *Time Team*, did not work. In fact, there are a lot of circumstances where they are not suitable at all.

I met the Council representative who looked after the cemeteries and I was *driven*, yes, it was that big, to the area concerned. In front of me was a piece of land about the size of a football pitch with a few rose beds scattered about and mainly laid to grass. I began at a point where some gravestones still stood in order to get myself tuned in to grave sites. After plotting out the size of one or two with headstones, I then moved out onto the open ground. I decided to move diagonally across the area as graves are usually in lines and if I started to dowse and picked up the paths between graves I would not find them as they would be either side of me. Abutting the visible graves there did seem to be others which, over time, had been obliterated, but eventually I came to an area which seemed free.

The border line was irregular but some yellow spray paint was put down to mark the perimeter of an area in which the garden of remembrance could be laid. It was quite interesting that where some graves had been lost, there was a section without burials. This area formed a circle about 20 feet in diameter, as though a memorial had been there. As it was outside my brief, I did not start looking for that particular aspect.

Double checking the area, I then returned to the visible headstones to confirm that I was still tuning in to burials and as it seemed I was, I felt confident enough to let the Borough Council take over.

Being a member of the BSD Council, a professional dowser and an approved tutor for them, you become aware of its operational scope. The view that it is just some old boy with a forked stick trying to pull the wool over the eyes of a credulous public, could not be further from the truth. As I have stated before, most members are highly intelligent and those that aren't particularly academic have an ability which has come naturally to them.

We all start off as non-dowsers who by chance find that things happen when we use rods, a forked stick or a pendulum. Our curiosity pushes us on and I am sure most of us are somewhat cautious about what is happening and why. For that reason, it is important to get proof that what we are finding does exist and that we are not just deluding ourselves.

There are people out there who say they can dowse but sometimes it is a vivid imagination at play. These characters bring dowsing into disrepute which is why the BSD has a register of approved dowsers to whom members of the public can be referred.

Some dowsers are good at one particular aspect, for example, finding objects lost at home or in a garden. Even working from a sketch of a property, they are often successful, yet it is something I have great difficulty with. By the same token, I can map dowse anywhere in the world for water and archaeological sites and have a good success rate. No one gets it right all the time, in the same way that electronic instruments will fail occasionally.

If you can dowse for one thing there is no reason why it should not be possible to find other things, but if you have a seeming affinity with one particular aspect, everything seems to work better.

The BSD runs a series of dowsing courses each year on many different aspects, so if your interests are as diverse as mine, there will be a course for you. If you *want* to do it, there is every chance you will master the subject eventually. Sometimes things just fall into place and other times you have to go back to it time and time again. One day when you are in a really relaxed state it will just happen and that is a moment to savour.

In my own case, curiosity drew me on and, with encouragement from other dowsers, it has been a life-changing experience. How does it work? Learn to dowse and you will find out!

As a BSD approved tutor, I take fellow dowsers and learners on courses from time to time which is really enjoyable, and there is always the possibility of a problem cropping up.

Last year, for example, I was running a course at an agricultural college with the idea that on day one, everyone would go to a pre-planned site where other dowsers had picked up something in the past, but where no real follow up had taken place.

The weather had been hot for weeks and with about ten people to guide, they seemed to be doing well. The idea was that on the second day a JCB would be employed to move away the top soil to check if the dowsing was accurate. This was a first for the BSD to dowse and dig over one weekend so that people could get immediate feedback as to their abilities.

Day one was accomplished without any problem but in the evening I was told that the father of next day's JCB driver had had a stroke. Understandably our driver needed to be with his father in the hospital and not with us. There was no chance of getting another driver at such short notice. The next question was, "Could we physically dig part of the area?"

Going back to the site, we had to choose a couple of small squares to home in on but the ground was rock hard. However, a hosepipe from a local house was available and the owner offered to run water over the area until very late. We also had access to some shovels, forks, picks and spades, so we still stood a chance.

The next morning was hot and sunny. When we got back to the site, the ground was soaking wet but hopes soon evaporated when the first fork was pushed into the ground. After about two inches we were back to a concrete-like consistency and despite a lot of effort, had to admit defeat.

Although running a course means you have a number of dowsers working together, dowsers work best when they are on their own. Concentration is better and there is nobody to influence your thoughts. Like painters asked to paint a scene, they all look at the same view, but their paintings can vary considerably.

I was asked recently to visit a Napoleonic fort with the intention of maybe finding old tunnels which had either been filled in or forgotten about. It was a big site so I asked a couple of my colleagues to come with me but they were delayed, so while waiting for them, I sat down with a cup of tea.

The fort was having an open day with all sorts of events going on and as I sat there, coming across the parade ground in two very straight lines was a group of youngsters, no more than seven or eight years old, in British Army redcoat uniforms with hats and plastic guns, being marched by an adult. All was well until the command HALT was given. The boys at the front stopped, but those behind who were busy talking, didn't, and there was only what could be described as a rolling shunt as hats and guns went all over the place. However, they got themselves sorted out and standing smartly in two lines once again looked fine until the command ABOUT TURN was given. At this point, some turned one way, some another and the rest just stood, completely nonplussed. Eventually, they all turned and off they marched, seemingly having the time of their lives.

I mention this because, wherever you go dowsing, some sort of event seems to be taking place. The tunnels at this fort, if they are there, will take some working on and this is very much work in hand.

Colonel John Blashford-Snell OBE
Expedition Base
Motcombe
Shaftesbury
Dorset SP7 9PB
England

Email: jbs@ses-explore.org
Internet: http://www.ses-explore.org

THE SCIENTIFIC
EXPLORATION
SOCIETY

Tel:
Fax:

Global Expeditions:
Tel: 01747 854898

12 March 2007

John Baker Esq
68 Ironmill Lane
Crayford
Kent
DA1 4RR

Dear John

We are most grateful to you for so kindly coming to Motcombe to assist the Kota Mama VI project in Bolivia. Your advice and instruction was much appreciated and we look forward to examining the possible locations of rock that you indicated on the satellite photos.

It was marvellous that James took to dowsing so quickly and I'm sure this will stand him in good stead in his life as a Sapper Officer.

Yours stories of dowsing were fascinating. We talked about them long after you had headed back to Kent.

Thank you so much for your help. We look forward to seeing you on 16th April at the launch of the project in London.

With best wishes for successful dowsing.

Yours ever
John

John Blashford-Snell

CHAPTER TWENTY-NINE

Dowsing for meteorites

Speaking of work in hand, this is very much the case regarding my involvement with Col John Blashford-Snell and his recent expedition to Bolivia in search of a meteorite crater. My part in this was to map dowse satellite photographs and look for core remains and any sub-surface minerals thrown up or created by the impact.

As in all walks of life, the more contacts you have, the more you get and in the case of dowsing, contacts can come from a bewildering variety of areas, which makes this particular interest all the more exciting.

It was one of these contacts, Anne Leonard, who was on the BSD Council with me, who put me in contact with John whom you may recall ran a scientific expedition *Operation Raleigh*, some years back. He was setting up another expedition, *Kota Mama V1* to Bolivia, and it was suggested that I would be a likely help in doing some map dowsing for him prior to departure.

The reason dowsing was so readily accepted by SES is that John used dowsing himself when he was in the Royal Engineers.

While it does not work every time – what does? – it can save a lot of leg-work. When I heard what the terrain was like in this particular area of Bolivia, I did not feel any urge to rush to my nearest travel agency. Instead I was invited down to the headquarters of John's organisation, the Scientific Exploration Society (SES) at Motcombe in Dorset, not really knowing what I was in for but curious to say the least.

I was greeted by John, Anne and Yoli, who looked after the South American side of SES. Yoli was the first Inca lady I had ever met, and we all had dinner together that evening. On the following day we went into the expedition offices where I was shown satellite photographs of an area of Bolivia that looked to be completely forested with the occasional river meandering through it.

There was also a feature which was circular in shape, the spot the expedition was hoping to reach.The question was this: is this the site of a very old meteorite strike, and if so, what could I find out about it? The first thing I had to do was dowse to see if it was a meteorite crater at all, and having received a yes answer, I set about the next part of the exercise. It's not every day you're asked to look for meteorites and it presented something of a challenge, but as I know nothing about them, at least I could dowse without any preconceptions, which is the first rule of dowsing.

Working my way across the map, I was looking for anomalies in the ground such as rock that had been forced to the surface by a huge impact. The crater was six miles across and slowly, outcrops of rock started to show around two sides of the perimeter, which I duly marked. This rock might contain ore or precious metals and, with Bolivia being such a poor country, if there was anything of value, it could be exploited.

Eventually I had marked the relevant places on which the expedition could home in. The next question was, where was the core of what remained of the meteorite? Working my way across the circular feature I could find nothing, but then I was told meteorites rarely hit the earth at a 90º angle. So widening my search I eventually picked up what seemed to be its remains some two miles north of the crater. Job done for me but just the start for *Kota Mama V1*.

The expedition set off in mid-2007 and you can find out what happened at www.ses-explore.org/Page1.aspx?PageID=2022

Note: Since writing the above, I have learned it is now 99 per cent certain that it *was* a meteorite hit, some 5–6 thousand years ago.

Chapter Thirty

Dowsing makes you think

Since that fateful day some twelve or so years ago when I first held a pair of dowsing rods, all sorts of amazing things have happened to me. When I first met Dan Wilson, one of the things he said was that if I continued, it would change my life and my attitude to life. I have to say he was right. I see things more clearly and sometimes I am aware of things which are missed by other people. Dowsing certainly boosts the confidence and other dowsers get the same effect.

The people I meet as a direct result of all this are, without exception, very nice human beings, and fascinating in their own right. The apparent coincidences that happen are seemingly more plentiful than you would normally expect and wherever I have been, doors seem to have just opened up in front of me. It's a bit like Alice falling down the rabbit hole and there's a good way to go yet.

The other thing that has helped me is that when I first started out, I was very much on my own. It did me no harm as it made me think things through for myself, and I've since come to realise DOWSING MAKES YOU THINK! I put that in capitals because all we seem to do today is press buttons and answers pop up, we don't engage our brains let alone our subconscious, which is where so much information is stored and where dowsers go – amongst other places – to find the answers to their questions.

As mentioned before, a lot of BSD members have letters after their names and yet non-dowsing academics seem to have a great deal of trouble getting their heads round the phenomenon. Some are scared of the subject, dismiss it as rubbish or mumbo jumbo, yet I, and others like me, have plenty of cast-iron evidence that it works.

Life is too short to waste it on self-delusion. At this point in my journey, the BSD is getting its act together and new life is being put into it. No longer a little outpost of dowsing, the London Group has another twenty-plus other groups to make contact with throughout the UK, with a central office in Malvern which gives excellent back-up when needed.

As to what will happen next, whatever it is it will be unexpected, interesting and a challenge. The most exciting adventure we can have is when we travel through our own minds, finding out about ourselves and seeing the world in a totally different light. That's dowsing. Try it.

CHAPTER THIRTY-ONE

Things to try at home

Small beginnings

Place two chairs beside each other and ask a male and a female to sit on them. Now approach them from behind with your dowsing rods above their heads in the find position, concentrating first on one person and then the other.

As you reach the top of his or her head, the rods will either open or close. With me, they cross for a man and open for a woman. Positive and negative, yin and yang. You may get a different reaction, but you should get a very definite response.

A simple search

In this sequence, a dowser is looking for a copper pipe *(See colour plate section*). She is standing with the rods (made of any metal) in the find position.

As she gets nearer to the pipe, the rods start to cross and are at right angles to her body when she is over what she is looking for. As she walks on, the rods begin to uncross and will eventually open up as in the first picture.

Beginners often get a 'late' response and in those situations you carry out the same procedure but from the other side of the pipe. This will give you two find positions and the pipe should be between the two.

Dowsing for water

Here is something you can try if you live in a house with a front garden. Usually the mains water supply comes in from the road to the front of the house. Walk across the front garden with a pair of dowsing rods in the find position. Imagine you are looking for a water pipe. As you get near it, the rods will start to move, usually inwards but sometimes outwards. When they have travelled through 90 degrees (wide open or crossed), that should be the point where the water pipe enters the house. If you carry on walking, the rods will come back to the find position. You can then follow the line of the pipe to the stop-cock.

Psychometry

When I cross a field looking for, say, an eighteenth-century building foundation, if it's there, I will find it, but if there are foundations from another century, I won't find them until I actually start to ask for those periods. Yet nature does not have a timescale as such. These dates are applied by mankind to give an historical perspective to an event or chain of events. So why is it that by 'tuning in' to a particular century, all other centuries are omitted from my thought processes?

Map dowsing

Map dowsing is an ability to find people (providing you ask their permission first) and anything else you may wish to find, anywhere in the world, just by sitting at home with a map, plan or in some cases a sketch of what or who you are looking for. These are things that many dowsers can do and get results, but you have to ask, where does this information come from?

Conclusion

Dowsing raises some profound questions and I find that the answers to some of them are quite astounding and life-changing. Every dowser has to go on this journey of discovery for him/herself and come to their own conclusions.

Having spoken to fellow dowsers about this, their experiences are remarkably similar. The journey begins, in the UK at least, with the British Society of Dowsers. A visit to their website - www.britishdowsers.org - will enable you to find your nearest dowsing group, which is a good place to begin.